MASTER THE™ DSST

Business Mathematics Exam

PETERSON'S®

About Peterson's

Peterson's® has been your trusted educational publisher for over 50 years. It's a milestone we're quite proud of, as we continue to offer the most accurate, dependable, high-quality educational content in the field, providing you with everything you need to succeed. No matter where you are on your academic or professional path, you can rely on Peterson's for its books, online information, expert test-prep tools, the most up-to-date education exploration data, and the highest quality career success resources—everything you need to achieve your education goals. For our complete line of products, visit www.petersons.com.

For more information, contact Peterson's, 8740 Lucent Blvd., Suite 400, Highlands Ranch, CO 80129; 800-338-3282 Ext. 54229; or find us online at **www.petersons.com**.

ISBN: 978-0-7689-4439-6

Printed in the United States of America

10 9 8 7 6 5 4 3 2 1   22 21 20

Contents

Before You Begin

HOW THIS BOOK IS ORGANIZED

Peterson's *Master the*™ *DSST*® *Business Mathematics Exam* provides a diagnostic test, subject-matter review, and a post-test.

- **Diagnostic Test**—Twenty multiple-choice questions, followed by an answer key with detailed answer explanations
- **Assessment Grid**—A chart designed to help you identify areas that you need to focus on based on your test results
- **Subject-Matter Review**—General overview of the exam subject, followed by a review of the relevant topics and terminology covered on the exam.
- **Post-test**—Sixty multiple-choice questions, followed by an answer key and detailed answer explanations

The purpose of the diagnostic test is to help you figure out what you know—or don't know. The twenty multiple-choice questions are similar to the ones found on the DSST exam, and they should provide you with a good idea of what to expect. Once you take the diagnostic test, check your answers to see how you did. Included with each correct answer is a brief explanation regarding why a specific answer is correct, and in many cases, why other options are incorrect. Use the assessment grid to identify the questions you miss so that you can spend more time reviewing that information later. As with any exam, knowing your weak spots greatly improves your chances of success.

Following the diagnostic test is a subject-matter review. The review summarizes the various topics covered on the DSST exam. Key terms are defined; important concepts are explained; and when appropriate, examples are provided. As you read the review, some of the information may seem familiar while other information may seem foreign. Again, take note of the unfamiliar because that will most likely cause you problems on the actual exam.

After studying the subject-matter review, you should be ready for the post-test. The post-test contains sixty multiple-choice items, and it will serve as a dry run for the real DSST exam. There are complete answer explanations at the end of the test.

OTHER DSST PRODUCTS BY PETERSON'S

Books, flashcards, practice tests, and videos available online at **www.petersons.com/testprep/dsst**

- Art of the Western World
- Astronomy
- Business Mathematics
- Business Ethics and Society
- Civil War and Reconstruction
- Computing and Information Technology
- Criminal Justice
- Environmental Science
- Ethics in America
- Ethics in Technology
- Foundations of Education
- Fundamentals of College Algebra
- Fundamentals of Counseling
- Fundamentals of Cybersecurity
- General Anthropology
- Health and Human Development
- History of the Soviet Union
- History of the Vietnam War
- Human Resource Management
- Introduction to Business
- Introduction to Geography
- Introduction to Geology
- Introduction to Law Enforcement
- Introduction to World Religions
- Lifespan Developmental Psychology
- Math for Liberal Arts
- Management Information Systems
- Money and Banking
- Organizational Behavior
- Personal Finance
- Principles of Advanced English Composition
- Principles of Finance
- Principles of Public Speaking
- Principles of Statistics
- Principles of Supervision
- Substance Abuse
- Technical Writing

Like what you see? Get unlimited access to Peterson's full catalog of DSST practice tests, instructional videos, flashcards, and more for **75% off the first month**! Go to **www.petersons.com/testprep/dsst** and use coupon code **DSST2020** at checkout. Offer expires July 1, 2021.

Chapter 1

All About the DSST® Exam

WHAT IS DSST®?

Previously known as the DANTES Subject Standardized Tests, the DSST program provides the opportunity for individuals to earn college credit for what they have learned outside of the traditional classroom. Accepted or administered at more than 1,900 colleges and universities nationwide and approved by the American Council on Education (ACE), the DSST program enables individuals to use the knowledge they have acquired outside the classroom to accomplish their educational and professional goals.

WHY TAKE A DSST® EXAM?

DSST exams offer a way for you to save both time and money in your quest for a college education. Why enroll in a college course in a subject you already understand? For more than 30 years, the DSST program has offered the perfect solution for individuals who are knowledgeable in a specific subject and want to save both time and money. A passing score on a DSST exam provides physical evidence to universities of proficiency in a specific subject. More than 1,900 accredited and respected colleges and universities across the nation award undergraduate credit for passing scores on DSST exams. With the DSST program, individuals can shave months off the time it takes to earn a degree.

The DSST program offers numerous advantages for individuals in all stages of their educational development:

- Adult learners
- College students
- Military personnel

Adult learners desiring college degrees face unique circumstances—demanding work schedules, family responsibilities, and tight budgets. Yet adult learners also have years of valuable work experience that can frequently be applied toward a degree through the DSST program. For example, adult learners with on-the-job experience in business and management might be able to skip the Business 101 courses if they earn passing marks on DSST exams such as Introduction to Business and Principles of Supervision.

Adult learners can put their prior learning into action and move forward with more advanced course work. Adults who have never enrolled in a college course may feel a little uncertain about their abilities. If this describes your situation, then sign up for a DSST exam and see how you do. A passing score may be the boost you need to realize your dream of earning a degree. With family and work commitments, adult learners often feel they lack the time to attend college. The DSST program provides adult learners with the unique opportunity to work toward college degrees without the time constraints of semester-long course work. DSST exams take two hours or less to complete. In one weekend, you could earn credit for multiple college courses.

The DSST exams also benefit students who are already enrolled in a college or university. With college tuition costs on the rise, most students face financial challenges. The fee for each DSST exam starts at $80 (plus administration fees charged by some testing facilities)—significantly less than the $750 average cost of a 3-hour college class. Maximize tuition assistance by taking DSST exams for introductory or mandatory course work. Once you earn a passing score on a DSST exam, you are free to move on to higher-level course work in that subject matter, take desired electives, or focus on courses in a chosen major.

Not only do college students and adult learners profit from DSST exams, but military personnel reap the benefits as well. If you are a member of the armed services at home or abroad, you can initiate your post-military career by taking DSST exams in areas with which you have experience. Military personnel can gain credit anywhere in the world, thanks to the fact that almost all the tests are available through the internet at designated testing locations. DSST testing facilities are located at more than 500 military installations, so service members on active duty can get a jump-start on a post-military career with the DSST program. As an additional incentive, DANTES (Defense Activity for Non-Traditional Education Support) provides funding for DSST test fees for eligible members of the military.

More than 30 subject-matter tests are available in the fields of Business, Humanities, Math, Physical Science, Social Sciences, and Technology.

Available DSST® Exams

Business	Social Sciences
Business Ethics and Society	A History of the Vietnam War
Business Mathematics	Art of the Western World
Computing and Information Technology	Criminal Justice
Human Resource Management	Foundations of Education
Introduction to Business	Fundamentals of Counseling
Management Information Systems	General Anthropology
Money and Banking	History of the Soviet Union
Organizational Behavior	Introduction to Geography
Personal Finance	Introduction to Law Enforcement
Principles of Finance	Lifespan Developmental Psychology
Principles of Supervision	Substance Abuse
	The Civil War and Reconstruction
Humanities	**Physical Sciences**
Ethics in America	Astronomy
Introduction to World Religions	Environment Science
Principles of Advanced English Composition	Health and Human Development
Principles of Public Speaking	Introduction to Geology
Math	**Technology**
Fundamentals of College Algebra	Ethics in Technology
Math for Liberal Arts	Fundamentals of Cybersecurity
Principles of Statistics	Technical Writing

As you can see from the table, the DSST program covers a wide variety of subjects. However, it is important to ask two questions before registering for a DSST exam.

1. Which universities or colleges award credit for passing DSST exams?
2. Which DSST exams are the most relevant to my desired degree and my experience?

Knowing which universities offer DSST credit is important. In all likelihood, a college in your area awards credit for DSST exams, but find out before taking an exam by contacting the university directly. Then review the list of DSST exams to determine which ones are most relevant to the degree you are seeking and to your base of knowledge. Schedule an appointment with your college adviser to determine which exams best fit your degree program and which college courses the DSST exams can replace. Advisers should also be able to tell you the minimum score required on the DSST exam to receive university credit.

DSST® TEST CENTERS

You can find DSST testing locations in community colleges and universities across the country. Check the DSST website (**www.getcollegecredit. com**) for a location near you or contact your local college or university to find out if the school administers DSST exams. Keep in mind that some universities and colleges administer DSST exams only to enrolled students. DSST testing is available to men and women in the armed services at more than 500 military installations around the world.

HOW TO REGISTER FOR A DSST® EXAM

Once you have located a nearby DSST testing facility, you need to contact the testing center to find out the exam administration schedule. Many centers are set up to administer tests via the internet, while others use printed materials. Almost all DSST exams are available as online tests, but the method used depends on the testing center. The cost for each DSST exam starts at $80, and many testing locations charge a fee to cover their costs for administering the tests. Credit cards are the only accepted payment method for taking online DSST exams. Credit card, certified check, and money order are acceptable payment methods for paper-and-pencil tests.

Test takers are allotted two score reports—one mailed to them and another mailed to a designated college or university, if requested. Online tests generate unofficial scores at the end of the test session, while individuals taking paper tests must wait four to six weeks for score reports.

PREPARING FOR A DSST® EXAM

Even though you are knowledgeable in a certain subject matter, you should still prepare for the test to ensure you achieve the highest score possible. The first step in studying for a DSST exam is to find out what will be on the specific test you have chosen. Information regarding test content is located on the DSST fact sheets, which can be downloaded at no cost from **www. getcollegecredit.com**. Each fact sheet outlines the topics covered on a subject-matter test, as well as the approximate percentage assigned to each topic. For example, questions on the Business Math exam are distributed in the following way: Number Sense—5%, Algebraic Concepts—16%, Statistics—14%, Business Applications—49%, Financial Mathematics—16%.

In addition to the breakdown of topics on a DSST exam, the fact sheet also lists recommended reference materials. If you do not own the recommended books, then check college bookstores. Avoid paying high prices for new textbooks by looking online for used textbooks. Don't panic if you are unable to locate a specific textbook listed on the fact sheet; the textbooks are merely recommendations. Instead, search for comparable books used in university courses on the specific subject. Current editions are ideal, and it is a good idea to use at least two references when studying for a DSST exam. Of course, the subject matter provided in this book will be a sufficient review for most test takers. However, if you need additional information, it is a good idea to have some of the reference materials at your disposal when preparing for a DSST exam.

Fact sheets include other useful information in addition to a list of reference materials and topics. Each fact sheet includes subject-specific sample questions like those you will encounter on the DSST exam. The sample questions provide an idea of the types of questions you can expect on the exam. Test questions are multiple-choice with one correct answer and three incorrect choices.

The fact sheet also includes information about the number of credit hours ACE has recommended be awarded by colleges for a passing DSST exam score. However, you should keep in mind that not all universities and colleges adhere to the ACE recommendation for DSST credit hours. Some institutions require DSST exam scores higher than the minimum score recommended by ACE. Once you have acquired appropriate reference materials and you have the outline provided on the fact sheet, you are ready to start studying, which is where this book can help.

TEST DAY

After reviewing the material and taking practice tests, you are finally ready to take your DSST exam. Follow these tips for a successful test day experience.

1. **Arrive on time.** Not only is it courteous to arrive on time to the DSST testing facility, but it also allows plenty of time for you to take care of check-in procedures and settle into your surroundings.
2. **Bring identification.** DSST test facilities require that candidates bring a valid government-issued identification card with a current photo and signature.

Acceptable forms of identification include a current driver's license, passport, military identification card, or state-issued identification card. Individuals who fail to bring proper identification to the DSST testing facility will not be allowed to take an exam.

3. **Bring the right supplies.** If your exam requires the use of a calculator, you may bring a calculator that meets the specifications. For paper-based exams, you may also bring No. 2 pencils with an eraser and black ballpoint pens. Regardless of the exam methodology, you are NOT allowed to bring reference or study materials, scratch paper, or electronics such as cell phones, personal handheld devices, cameras, alarm wrist watches, or tape recorders to the testing center.

4. **Take the test.** During the exam, take the time to read each question and the provided answers carefully. Eliminate the choices you know are incorrect to narrow the number of potential answers. If a question completely stumps you, take an educated guess and move on—remember that DSSTs are timed; you will have 2 hours to take the exam.

With the proper preparation, DSST exams will save you both time and money. So join the thousands of people who have already reaped the benefits of DSST exams and move closer than ever to your college degree.

BUSINESS MATHEMATICS EXAM FACTS

The DSST Business Mathematics exam was developed to enable schools to award credit to students for knowledge equivalent to that learned by students taking the course. This exam contains 80 questions to be answered in 2 hours and covers topics such as number sense, algebraic concepts, statistics, and business applications.

The use of a non-programmable calculator is permitted in this exam.

Area or Course Equivalent: Business Mathematics
Level: Lower-level baccalaureate
Amount of Credit: 3 Semester Hours
Minimum Score: 400
Source: https://www.getcollegecredit.com/wp-content/assets/factsheets /BusinessMathematics.pdf

I. Number Sense – 5%

    a. Percentages, Fractions, and Decimals

II. Algebraic Concepts – 16%

    a. Linear equations and inequalities

    b. Simultaneous linear equations

    c. Quadratic equations and functions

    d. Graphing equations and evaluating functions

III. Statistics – 14%

    a. Central tendency

    b. Expected value

    c. Weighted averages

    d. Dispersion

    e. Probability distributions

    f. Percentiles

IV. Business Applications – 49%

    a. Index numbers

    b. Interest

    c. Depreciation / salvage value

    d. Discounts and credit terms

    e. Installment purchases, promissory notes and other loans

    f. Markup/markdown

    g. Taxes (e.g., Payroll, income, sales tax, property tax)

    h. Cost calculations (e.g., gross and net pay, fixed and variable costs)

    i. Break-even analysis (algebraically and graphically)

    j. Financial ratio calculation and analysis

    k. Interpretation of graphical representations (and misuse of data)

    l. Extrapolation and Interpolation

   m. Unit conversions (e.g., currency)

   n. Investment performance measures (e.g., p/e ratios, yield factors, rates of return)

    o. Cost minimization/value optimization

    p. Inventory valuation

V. Financial Mathematics – 16%

    a. Annuities and present value

    b. Amortization and future value

    c. Annual percentage rate

    d. Effective annual rate

Chapter 2

Business Mathematics Diagnostic Test

DIAGNOSTIC TEST ANSWER SHEET

1. Ⓐ Ⓑ Ⓒ Ⓓ

2. Ⓐ Ⓑ Ⓒ Ⓓ

3. Ⓐ Ⓑ Ⓒ Ⓓ

4. Ⓐ Ⓑ Ⓒ Ⓓ

5. Ⓐ Ⓑ Ⓒ Ⓓ

6. Ⓐ Ⓑ Ⓒ Ⓓ

7. Ⓐ Ⓑ Ⓒ Ⓓ

8. Ⓐ Ⓑ Ⓒ Ⓓ

9. Ⓐ Ⓑ Ⓒ Ⓓ

10. Ⓐ Ⓑ Ⓒ Ⓓ

11. Ⓐ Ⓑ Ⓒ Ⓓ

12. Ⓐ Ⓑ Ⓒ Ⓓ

13. Ⓐ Ⓑ Ⓒ Ⓓ

14. Ⓐ Ⓑ Ⓒ Ⓓ

15. Ⓐ Ⓑ Ⓒ Ⓓ

16. Ⓐ Ⓑ Ⓒ Ⓓ

17. Ⓐ Ⓑ Ⓒ Ⓓ

18. Ⓐ Ⓑ Ⓒ Ⓓ

19. Ⓐ Ⓑ Ⓒ Ⓓ

20. Ⓐ Ⓑ Ⓒ Ⓓ

BUSINESS MATHEMATICS DIAGNOSTIC TEST

Directions: Carefully read each of the following 20 questions. Choose the best answer to each question and fill in the corresponding circle on the answer sheet. The Answer Key and Explanations can be found following this Diagnostic Test.

1. Use the quadratic equation to solve for x where $x^2 + 4x - 21$.

   A. $-2 \pm 2\sqrt{17}$

   B. $3, -7$

   C. $3, 7$

   D. $-3, \ 2 + 2\sqrt{17}$

2. The science teacher asked each student in the science class to measure the temperature in degrees Fahrenheit for the classroom. For various reasons, not all of the students came up with the same answer. The students' measurements were 72, 74, 72, 70, 68, and 76. What was the mean ± the standard deviation?

   A. $72 \pm 2\sqrt{2}$

   B. $72 \pm 4\sqrt{2}$

   C. 72 ± 8

   D. 74 ± 8

3. A data set consists of the values (45, 3, 7, 26, 12, 9, 57, 3, 12). Which number in the group would be the value of the lowest quartile?

   A. 3

   B. 7

   C. 9

   D. 12

4. The number of people employed by the city in 1990 was 220. In 2000, there were 440 employees. In 2010, the number had grown to 880. What is the index number for city employment in 2000 relative to 1990?

A. 4
B. 20
C. 400
D. 800

5. A semiconductor company buys a tool for 2 million dollars and will depreciate it over five years. Its residual value is $500,000. How much does the tool depreciate per year?

A. $100,000
B. $300,000
C. $400,000
D. $500,000

6. Janet purchases a vacuum for $1,500 from a janitorial supply store. The credit terms are 5/10, *n*/20. How much would she pay if she paid her bill in 15 days?

A. $75
B. $1,487
C. $1,475
D. $1,500

7. Sarah marked up the prices of dresses in her shop. Her average selling price is $80 per dress, and her average cost is $60. What is her average % markup?

A. 20%
B. 33%
C. 66%
D. 75%

8. A town's budget is $600,000. The total assessed property value is 30 million dollars. What tax rate can the city council choose so that it raises exactly the amount it needs for the city's budget?

A. 2%
B. 3%
C. 4%
D. 20%

9. Colleen is in charge of selling calendars. The cost equation for her company's newest calendar is $C(x) = 0.5x + 1,000$ in dollars. For what price must she sell the calendars, if she wishes to break even at 1,000 units?

   A. $1.50
   B. $2
   C. $15
   D. $1,500

10. If the total cost for manufacturing large screen TVs is $C(x) = 200x + 50,000$ in dollars, what is the fixed cost to manufacture 500 TVs?

    A. $200
    B. $50,000
    C. $100,000
    D. $150,000

11. Solve the equation for q, where $5q - 3 = 7$.

    A. $\dfrac{4}{5}$
    B. 2
    C. 5
    D. 7

12. Martin purchased a new truck for $15,000 on an installment plan. He agreed to pay $300 monthly for 5 years with a down payment of $500. What is the deferred payment price for Martin's truck?

    A. $18,500
    B. $20,000
    C. $22,500
    D. $24,500

13. A woman takes out a loan from her local bank for $1,000. She will repay the money in two years at a rate of 10%. How much interest will she pay?

    A. $20
    B. $200
    C. $2,000
    D. $20,000

14. A large group of sales people attended a weekend sales conference, where an 18-round golf tournament was held in the afternoon. The winner of the tournament shot a 72, but his boss had the worst score of the day at 114. The average score was a 94, with most golfers scoring a 96. What was the mode score for the tournament?

    A. 42
    B. 94
    C. 95
    D. 96

15. Tara created the following trend analysis table to track her company's cookie sales. Her base year for comparison was 2016, when the company sold $40,000 in cookies. What was the company's sales for 2015?

Year:	2015	2016	2017	2018
Sales:	90%	100%	120%	80%

    A. $26,000
    B. $30,000
    C. $36,000
    D. $40,000

16. Which type of loan requires periodic payments with a final payment at the end of the loan period?

    A. Adjustable loan
    B. Single payment loan
    C. Balloon payment loan
    D. Noninterest bearing simple loan

17. A woman has $3 in quarters and dimes. She notices that she has twice as many quarters as dimes. How many quarters and how many dimes does she have?

    A. 5 dimes, 10 quarters
    B. 10 dimes, 8 quarters
    C. 3 dimes, 6 quarters
    D. None of the above

18. What would be the monthly payment if you borrowed $25,000 for five years at 6% annual interest?

A. $483.32
B. $523.56
C. $635.55
D. $695.76

19. Jonah wishes to save for his daughter's college fund. If he deposits $200 at the end of each month and earns 6.0% compounded monthly for 18 years, how much will he have in his account at the end of this time?

A. $71,112.67
B. $73,118.80
C. $75,120.45
D. $77,470.64

20. A test was given to 480 students and 468 passed. What percentage of students did NOT pass the test?

A. 0.025%
B. 2.5%
C. 0.975%
D. 97.5%

ANSWER KEY AND EXPLANATIONS

1. B	**5.** B	**9.** A	**13.** B	**17.** A
2. A	**6.** D	**10.** B	**14.** D	**18.** A
3. B	**7.** B	**11.** B	**15.** C	**19.** D
4. C	**8.** A	**12.** A	**16.** C	**20.** B

1. The correct answer is B. Using the quadratic equation with $a = 1$, $b = 4$, and $c = -21$:

$$x = \frac{-(4) \pm \sqrt{(4)^2 - 4(1)(-21)}}{2(1)}$$

$$x = \frac{-4 \pm \sqrt{16 + 84}}{2}$$

$$x = \frac{-4\sqrt{100}}{2}$$

$$x = \frac{-4 + 10}{2}$$

Now solve for both the negative and the positive solution:

$$x = \frac{-4 + 10}{2} \qquad x = \frac{-4 - 10}{2}$$

$$x = \frac{6}{2} \qquad x = \frac{-14}{2}$$

$$x = 3 \qquad x = -7$$

The answer is $x = 3, -7$.

2. **The correct answer is A.** First, calculate the mean:

$$\text{avg} = \frac{72 + 74 + 72 + 70 + 68 + 76}{6}$$

$$\text{avg} = \frac{432}{6}$$

$$\text{avg} = 72$$

Next, use the equation for standard deviation:

$$stdev = \sqrt{\sum_{i=1}^{n} \frac{(x_i - \bar{x})^2}{n-1}}$$

$$= \sqrt{\frac{(72-72)^2 + (74-72)^2 + (72-72)^2 + (70-72)^2 + (68-72)^2 + (76-72)^2}{6-1}}$$

$$= \sqrt{\frac{0 + 4 + 0 + 4 + 16 + 16}{5}}$$

$$= \sqrt{\frac{40}{5}}$$

$$= \sqrt{8}$$

$$= \sqrt{(4)(2)}$$

$$= 2\sqrt{2}$$

The mean and standard deviation is $72 \pm 2\sqrt{2}$.

3. **The correct answer is B.** First, arrange the numbers from lowest to highest:

$$(3, 3, 7, 9, 12, 12, 26, 45, 57)$$

There are nine entries. Using the equation for percentile, find the value of the lowest quartile:

$$n = \frac{N}{100}p + 0.5$$

$$= \frac{9}{100}(25) + 0.5$$

$$= 2.25 + 0.5$$

$$= 2.75$$

Round this number to the nearest integer = 3. The third value in the ranked data is 7.

4. **The correct answer is C.** To calculate the index number, divide the number of employees in the year 2010 by those in 1990 and multiply by 100.

$$= \left(\frac{880}{220} \right) 100$$
$$= (4)100$$
$$= 400$$

The index is 400.

5. **The correct answer is B.** Use the equation:

$$\text{Depreciation} = \frac{\text{Cost} - \text{Residual Value}}{\text{Estimated Useful Life}}$$

And solve:

$$= \frac{2,000,000 - 500,000}{5}$$
$$= \frac{1,500,000}{5}$$
$$= 300,000$$

The tool depreciates $300,000 per year.

6. **The correct answer is D.** The 5/10 means a 5% discount if net is paid in 10 days. Otherwise, net is due in 20 days. Janet did not pay her bill in 10 days, so she receives no discount. She will pay the full amount.

7. The correct answer is B. Using the equation for Selling Price = (Total Cost)(1 + % markup). We can calculate the % markup as x:

$$80 = 60(1+x)$$
$$1+x = \frac{80}{60}$$
$$x = \frac{80}{60} - 1$$
$$x = \frac{4}{3} - 1$$
$$x = \frac{4}{3} - \frac{3}{3}$$
$$x = \frac{1}{3}$$
$$x = 33\%$$

The average markup is 33%.

8. The correct answer is A. Using the equation:

$$\text{Tax Rate} = \frac{\text{Budget Needed}}{\text{Total Assessed Value}}, \text{ solve for the tax rate:}$$

$$= \frac{600,000}{30,000,000}$$
$$= \frac{6}{300}$$
$$= \frac{1}{50}$$
$$= 0.020$$

The city will need a 2% tax rate.

9. The correct answer is A. To solve this problem, first set the cost of manufacturing equation equal to the equation for revenue. The equation for revenue is $R(x) = px$, where p is the price.

Set $x = 1,000$ and solve:

$$(p)(1,000) = 0.5(1,000) + 1,000$$
$$(p)(1,000) = 500 + 1,000$$
$$p = \frac{1,500}{1,000}$$
$$p = 1.5$$

Colleen must sell her calendars for $1.50.

10. **The correct answer is B.** The fixed cost does not change, no matter how many TVs are manufactured. If we set $x = 0$, we can see that the fixed cost is:

$$= 200(0) + 50,000$$
$$= 50,000$$

$50,000 is the fixed cost.

11. **The correct answer is B.** Solving linear equations requires that you isolate the variable q:

$$5q - 3 = 7$$
$$5q - 3 + 3 = 7 + 3$$
$$5q = 10$$
$$\frac{5q}{5} = \frac{10}{5}$$
$$q = 2$$

The value of q is 2.

12. **The correct answer is A.** The Deferred Payment Price = Total of All Payments + Down Payment. The total of all payments is (12)(5)(300) = $18,000. Add to this the $500 down payment and the total deferred payment price is $18,500.

13. **The correct answer is B.** To calculate interest, use the equation $i = PVrt$.

$$i = (1,000)(0.1)(2)$$
$$= 200$$

The woman will pay $200 in interest.

14. **The correct answer is D.** The mode is the most frequently occurring value and is stated to be 96.

15. The correct answer is C. To find the percentage, we divide the year's sales by the base year sales. We know $40,000 was the total sales in 2016, so we can solve where x = sales in 2015:

$$\frac{x}{40,000} = 0.9$$
$$x = 40,000(0.9)$$
$$x = 36,000$$

The company's sales in 2015 totaled $36,000.

16. The correct answer is C. A balloon payment requires periodic payments of principal and interest for a period of time. After the last payment is made, the remaining principal and interest are owed in one large payment.

17. The correct answer is A. Let q = the number of quarters and d = the number of dimes. We know that there are twice as many quarters as dimes.

$$q = 2d$$

We also know that the total number of dimes and quarters equals $3. We can solve for cents, so that we don't have to use decimals:

$$10d + 25q = 300$$

All that is required now is to substitute the first equation into the second and solve for the number of dimes:

$$10d + 25q = 300$$
$$10d + 25(2d) = 300$$
$$10d + 50d = 300$$
$$60d = 300$$
$$d = 5$$

If there are 5 dimes, then, using the first equation, we know there are 10 quarters.

18. The correct answer is A. Use the equation

$$PMT_{Amort} = \frac{PV\left(\dfrac{r}{m}\right)}{1-\left(1+\dfrac{r}{m}\right)^{-mt}} \text{ to solve:}$$

$$
\begin{aligned}
PMT_{Amort} &= \frac{25,000\left(\dfrac{0.06}{12}\right)}{1-\left(1+\dfrac{0.06}{12}\right)^{-(5)(12)}} \\[2mm]
&= \frac{25,000(0.005)}{1-(1+0.005)^{-60}} \\[2mm]
&= \frac{125}{1-(1.005)^{60}} \\[2mm]
&= \frac{125}{1-0.741372} \\[2mm]
&= 483.32
\end{aligned}
$$

The monthly payment is $483.32.

19. The correct answer is D. Use the equation

$$FV_{OA} = PMT\left[\frac{\left(1+\dfrac{r}{m}\right)^{tm}-1}{\dfrac{r}{m}}\right] \text{ to solve:}$$

$$
\begin{aligned}
&= 200\left[\frac{\left(1+\dfrac{0.06}{12}\right)^{216}-1}{\dfrac{0.06}{12}}\right] \\[2mm]
&= 200\left[\frac{\left(1+0.005\right)^{216}-1}{0.005}\right] \\[2mm]
&= 200\left[\frac{\left(1.005\right)^{216}-1}{0.005}\right] \\[2mm]
&= 200\left[\frac{2.936766-1}{0.005}\right] \\[2mm]
&= 77,470.64
\end{aligned}
$$

Jonah will save $77,470.64.

20. The correct answer is B. First, you need to find the number of students who didn't pass:

$$480 - 468 = 12$$

Next, divide the number of students who did not pass by the total number of students. Multiply this number by 100 to make it a percentage:

$$= \left(\frac{12}{480}\right)100$$
$$= (0.025)100$$
$$= 2.5\%$$

2.5% of the students did not pass the test.

DIAGNOSTIC TEST ASSESSMENT GRID

Now that you've completed the diagnostic test and read through the answer explanations, you can use your results to target your studying. Find the question numbers from the diagnostic test that you answered incorrectly and highlight or circle them below. Then focus extra attention on the sections dealing with those topics.

Business Mathematics		
Content Area	**Topic**	**Question #**
Number Sense	• Percentages, Fractions, and Decimals	15, 20
Algebraic Concepts	• Linear equations and inequalities • Simultaneous linear equations • Quadratic equations and functions • Graphing equations and evaluating functions	1, 11, 17
Statistics	• Central tendency • Expected value • Weighted averages • Dispersion • Probability distributions • Percentiles	2, 3, 14
Business Applications	• Index numbers • Interest • Depreciation / salvage value • Discounts and credit terms • Installment purchases, promissory notes and other loans • Markup/markdown • Taxes (e.g., Payroll, income, sales tax, property tax) • Cost calculations (e.g., gross and net pay, fixed and variable costs) • Break-even analysis (algebraically and graphically) • Financial ratio calculation and analysis • Interpretation of graphical representations (and misuse of data) • Extrapolation and Interpolation • Unit conversions (e.g., currency) • Investment performance measures (e.g., p/e ratios, yield factors, rates of return) • Cost minimization/value optimization • Inventory valuation	4, 5, 6, 7, 8, 9, 10

Financial Mathematics	• Annuities and present value	18, 19
	• Amortization and future value	
	• Annual percentage rate	
	• Effective annual rate	

Chapter 3

Business Mathematics Subject Review

NUMBER SENSE: PERCENTAGES, FRACTIONS, AND DECIMALS

When describing a baseball batting average, the chance of rain, or the odds of winning at poker, you are using a number to describe a part of a whole. There are three common ways to represent this relationship using numbers: **fractions**, **decimals**, and **percentages**.

The following are some examples:

- Fraction = $\frac{3}{4}$, 3/4 = three fourths, three over four, three divided by four, 3:4, three to four
- Decimal = 0.75 = zero point seven five, seventy-five hundredths, point seven five
- Percentage = 75% = seventy-five percent, 75 out of 100

The fraction 3/4 tells us that there are 3 equal parts of a whole that contains 4 total parts. It's important to remember that the top part of the fraction, 3 in this example, is called the **numerator**, and the bottom part, 4 in this example, is called the **denominator**.

When adding or subtracting fractions, the denominator must be the same number.

Multiplying by 1 expressed as the fraction $\frac{n}{n}$ can create the common denominator.

Example 1: Show use of $\frac{n}{n}$ to create a common denominator and to simplify.

Solution:

$$\text{Addition } \frac{3}{4}+\frac{1}{8}=\frac{3}{4}\left(\frac{2}{2}\right)+\frac{1}{8} \qquad \text{Reduction } \frac{10}{15}=\frac{(2)(5)}{(3)(5)}$$

$$=\frac{6}{8}+\frac{1}{8} \qquad\qquad =\frac{2}{3}\left(\frac{5}{5}\right)$$

$$=\frac{7}{8} \qquad\qquad\qquad =\frac{2}{3}$$

The decimal 0.75 tells us that there are 75 out of 100, or $75 \div 100 = 0.75$. Decimals are most commonly used in spreadsheets or when using calculators. Some fractions, such as $\frac{1}{3}$, are represented as a repeating decimal, or 0.333..., where the decimal is rounded up or down where appropriate. Sometimes, extra zeros are added to the end of decimals. For example, 0.750 means 750 out of 1,000. The extra zero doesn't change the value of the decimal.

Percentage means "per cent" or "out of 100." For example, 45% means 45 out of 100. To convert a decimal to a percentage, you must multiply the decimal by 100.

Example 2: A pie has 2 pieces left out of an original 8 pieces. Determine what percentage of the pie is left.

Solution: 2 out of $8 = \frac{2}{8}$, or $\frac{1}{4}$, $1 \div 4 = 0.25$, $0.25 \times 100 = 25\%$

ALGEBRAIC CONCEPTS

Linear Equations and Inequalities

Algebraic expressions are usually used to form **equations**, which set two expressions equal to each other. Equations contain at least one **variable**: a letter such as x or y that represents a number that can vary. Most equations you'll see on the exam are **linear equations**, in which the variables don't come with exponents.

To find the value of a linear equation's variable (such as x) is to **solve the equation**. To solve any linear equation containing only one variable, your goal is always the same: isolate the variable on one side of the equation.

The best way to do this is to isolate the variable on the left-hand side of the equation using addition, subtraction, multiplication, or division.

Whatever operation you perform on one side of an equation you must also perform on the other side; otherwise, the two sides won't be equal. Performing any of these operations on *both* sides does not change the equality; it merely restates the equation in a different form.

Solving an Equation Using the Four Basic Operations

To find the value of the variable (to solve for x), you may need to either add a term to both sides of the equation or subtract a term from both sides. Here are two examples:

Example 3: Solve the linear equation $x - 2 = 5$.

Solution: To solve, add the same number to both sides to find the value of x.

$$x - 2 = 5$$
$$x - 2 + 2 = 5 + 2$$
$$x = 7$$

Example 4: Solve the equation $\frac{3}{2} - x = 12$

Solution: The objective is to isolate the variable x. You will need to subtract the same number from both sides. To do this, like terms must be combined.

$$\frac{3}{2} - x = 12$$
$$-\frac{3}{2} \qquad -\frac{3}{2}$$
$$-x = 10\frac{1}{2} \quad \text{(divide by} -1 \text{ to make the variable positive)}$$
$$x = -10\frac{1}{2}$$

The first equation isolates x by adding 2 to both sides. The second equation isolates x by subtracting $\frac{3}{2}$ from both sides.

In some cases, solving for x requires that you either multiply or divide both sides of the equation by the same term. Here are two examples:

Example 5: Solve: $\frac{x}{2} = 14$

Solution: Multiply both sides by the same number:

$$\frac{x}{2} = 14$$

$$2 \times \frac{x}{2} - 14 \times 2$$

$$x = 28$$

Example 6: Solve for x: $3x = 18$

Solution: Divide both sides by the same number:

$$3x = 18$$

$$\frac{3x}{3} = \frac{18}{3}$$

$$x = 6$$

The first equation isolates x by multiplying 2 to both sides. The second equation isolates x by dividing both sides by 3.

If the variable appears on both sides of the equation, first perform whatever operation is required to position the variable on just one side—either the left or the right.

Example 7: Solve: $16 - x = 9 + 2x$

Solution: Position both x-terms on the left side by subtracting $2x$ from both sides:

$$16 - x = 9 + 2x$$

$$16 - x - 2x = 9 + 2x - 2x$$

$$16 - 3x - 9$$

Now that x appears on just one side, the next step is to isolate it by subtracting 16 from both sides, and then dividing both sides by -3:

$$16 - 3x = 9$$

$$16 - 3x - 16 = 9 - 16$$

$$-3x = -7$$

$$\frac{-3x}{-3} = \frac{-7}{-3}$$

$$x = \frac{7}{3}$$

An **inequality** is a math statement that, instead of an equal sign, uses one of the following: a "greater than" symbol (>), a "less than" symbol (<), a "greater than or equal to" symbol (≥), or a "less than or equal to" symbol (≤). Solving inequalities is very similar to solving linear equalities except for one simple rule:

Inequality Rule: The inequality sign must be flipped whenever you multiply or divide by a negative number. Expressed in symbolic form: if $a > b$, then $-a < -b$.

The following simple example demonstrates this important rule:

$12 - 4x < 8$ (original inequality)

$-4x < -4$ (subtract 12 from both sides; inequality unchanged)

$x > 1$ (both sides divided by -4; inequality reversed)

Here are some additional rules for dealing with algebraic inequalities.

1. Adding or subtracting unequal quantities to (or from) equal quantities:
   If $a > b$, then $c + a > c + b$

2. Adding unequal quantities to unequal quantities:
   If $a > b$, and if $c > d$, then $a + c > b + d$

3. Comparing three unequal quantities:
   If $a > b$, and if $b > c$, then $a > c$

4. Combining the same positive quantity with unequal quantities by multiplication or division:
   If $a > b$, and if $x > 0$, then $xa > xb$

   If $a > b$, and if $x > 0$, then $\dfrac{a}{x} > \dfrac{b}{x}$

   If $a > b$, and if $x > 0$, then $\dfrac{x}{a} < \dfrac{x}{b}$

5. Combining the same negative quantity with unequal quantities by multiplication or division:
   If $a > b$, and if $x < 0$, then $xa < xb$

   If $a > b$, and if $x < 0$, then $\dfrac{a}{x} < \dfrac{b}{x}$

   If $a > b$, and if $x < 0$, then $\dfrac{x}{a} > \dfrac{x}{b}$

Example 8: Solve $-3 - 5x < 7$.

Solution:

$$-3 - 5x < 7$$
$$-3 - 5x + 3 < 7 + 3$$
$$-5x < 10$$
$$-5x\left(\frac{1}{-5}\right) > 10\left(\frac{1}{-5}\right)$$
$$x > -2$$

Notice that the < sign was reversed because we multiplied by a negative number to isolate x.

Simultaneous Linear Equations

Many problems will require you to deal with more than one equation having more than one variable, which are called **simultaneous equations**. The goal is to find the values for the variables that make the equation true.

There are several ways to solve simultaneous equations. The easiest, and probably the most popular, method is the **substitution method**. This method involves using the following procedure:

Step 1: Solve one equation for one of the variables in terms of the other variable.

Step 2: Substitute the equation from Step 1 into the other equation, resulting in an equation that contains only one variable.

Step 3: Find the solution to the equation obtained in Step 2. This gives you the value of one variable.

Step 4: Use the value obtained in Step 3 in the remaining equation to solve for the second variable.

Example 9: Solve the simultaneous equations to find the values of x and y.

$$\begin{cases} 5x + y = 13 \\ x - 2y = 7 \end{cases}$$

Solution:

Step 1: We can solve the first equation for y. Subtract $5x$ from both sides:

$$5x + y = 13$$
$$5x + y - 5x = 13 - 5x$$
$$y = 13 - 5x$$

Step 2: Substitute this value of y into the second equation and solve for x:

$$x - 2y = 7$$
$$x - 2(13 - 5x) = 7$$

Step 3: Now solve the equation from Step 2:

$$x - 2(13 - 5x) = 7$$
$$x + (-2)(13) + (-2)(-5)x = 7$$
$$x - 26 + 10x = 7$$
$$(10 + 1)x - 26 = 7$$
$$11x - 26 + 26 = 7 + 26$$
$$11x = 33$$
$$x = 3$$

Step 4: Substitute this value of x into either equation (we'll use equation 2) and solve:

$$(3) - 2y = 7$$
$$3 - 2y - 3 = 7 - 3$$
$$-2y = 4$$
$$-2y\left(-\frac{1}{2}\right) = 4\left(\frac{1}{2}\right)$$
$$y = -2$$

Our solution is $x = 3$ and $y = -2$. Using substitution, we have shown how to solve simultaneous equations.

Quadratic Equations and Functions

A **quadratic expression** is one that contains a variable of the second order, or a squared variable. For example, $2x^2 - 3x + 5$ is a quadratic.

A **quadratic equation** is often solved by finding where the equation equals zero. An equation is quadratic if it can be expressed in the general form $ax^2 + bx + c = 0$. Every quadratic equation has exactly two solutions, called **roots** (But the two roots might be the same.). There are several ways to solve quadratic equations, but by far the easiest method involves using the quadratic formula.

If $ax^2 + bx + c = 0$, where $a \neq 0$, then the roots of the equation are given by:

$$x = \frac{-b \pm \sqrt{b^2 - 4ac}}{2a}$$

Example 10: Solve $2x^2 + 12x + 10 = 0$.

Solution: Letting $a = 2$, $b = 12$, and $c = 10$, we can solve:

$$x = \frac{-(12) \pm \sqrt{(12)^2 - 4(2)(10)}}{2(2)}$$

$$x = \frac{-12 \pm \sqrt{(12)^2 - 4(2)(10)}}{2(2)}$$

$$x = \frac{-12 \pm \sqrt{144 - 80}}{4}$$

$$x = \frac{-12 \pm \sqrt{64}}{4}$$

$$x = \frac{-12 \pm 8}{4}$$

Now solve for both the negative and positive solutions:

$$x = \frac{-12 + 8}{4} \qquad\qquad x = \frac{-12 - 8}{4}$$

$$x = \frac{-4}{4} \qquad\qquad x = \frac{-20}{4}$$

$$x = -1 \qquad\qquad x = -5$$

The answer is $x = -1$ and $x = -5$.

You may encounter other mathematical expressions, equations, and inequalities that involve exponents of order higher than 2. Table 1 contains rules for exponents that will assist you in solving these problems.

Table 1: Rules for Exponential Equations

Product	$a^m a^n = a^{m+n}$
Product of a power	$(a^m)^n = a^{mn}$
Quotient to a power	$\left(\dfrac{a}{b}\right)^n = \dfrac{a^n}{b^n}$
Quotient	$\dfrac{a^m}{a^n} = a^{m-n}$
Zero exponent	$a^0 = 1$
Negative exponent	$a^{-n} = \dfrac{1}{a^n}$
Inversion	$\left(\dfrac{a}{b}\right)^{-n} = \left(\dfrac{b}{a}\right)^n$

Functions

A **function** is a relationship between two quantities in which the value of one variable depends upon the value of, or is "a function of," another variable. The **domain** is the set of inputs that can be substituted in for the variable and produce a meaningful output. A function can have only one output for each input. If you are given a formula for a function, you can evaluate it at any value in its domain. Once you substitute a value for the variable, simplify the resulting numerical expression using the order of operations.

A function can be expressed using a table of values, a formula, or a graph. In mathematics, the relationship for a linear function is expressed in the form $y = f(x)$—where y is a function of x. The graph of a linear function is a straight line.

Observe the graph of a typical linear function $f(x) = mx + b$, where $m = 0$.

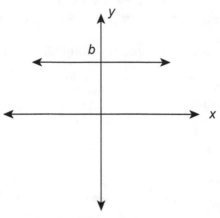

Figure 1

A **quadratic function** can be described by an equation of the form $f(x) = ax^2 + bx + c$, where $a \neq 0$. In a quadratic function, the greatest power of the variable is 2. The graph of a quadratic function is a parabola.

Observe the graph for the quadratic function $f(x) = ax^2 + bx + c$, where $a > 0$.

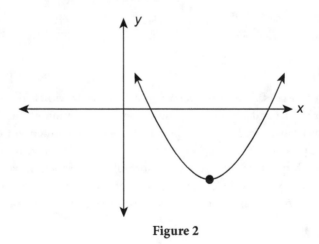

Figure 2

Graphing Equations and Evaluating Functions

Evaluating a function requires finding the values that are true for the function. In other words, substitute the input (the given number or expression) for the function's variable (x). Then replace the x with the number or expression.

For example, to evaluate $f(x) = -2x + 5$ at $x = -3$, substitute in -3 wherever there is an x term and then simplify:

$$f(-3) = -2(-3) + 5 = 6 + 5 = 11$$

Often you will evaluate a function or equation in order to graph the points so that you can know what the function looks like.

The steps for evaluating an equation to create a graph are as follows:

Step 1: Find ordered pairs that satisfy the equation. Pick values for x and solve for y. The best values to pick for x depend on the equation.

Step 2: Plot the values on the coordinate plane.

Step 3: Connect the dots to create the graph. If you don't have enough points to clearly graph the equation, create more pairs.

Connecting the Dots

To "connect the dots" when graphing a function may require that you construct new data points that fall within the existing range of data values. This technique is called **interpolation**. Interpolation often requires creating a missing value in a spreadsheet. For example, given the table below, you can identify the missing y_2-value with the equation provided. The only requirement is that the x and y data are both ranked in the same ascending or descending order:

x_1	y_1
x_2	
x_3	y_3

$$y_2 = \frac{(x_2 - x_1)(y_3 - y_1)}{(x_3 - x_1)} + y_1$$

If you needed to construct new data points outside the known data points, you would use **extrapolation**, which is estimation based on the trend of the existing data. Interpolations and extrapolation are often used when predicting trends and values in graphical representations for research, sales, and other business projections. These techniques will be discussed in this context later.

Example 11: Evaluate the function $f(x) = x^2 + 2x + 2$.

Step 1: Choose values for x and solve for $f(x)$ or y. Insert –3 into the equation and solve:

$$(-3)2 + 2(-3) + 2 = 5$$

Repeat for other points:

x	–5	–1	0	1	2
y	5	1	2	5	10

Steps 2 and 3: Graph the points and draw a fitted curve using extrapolation and interpolation:

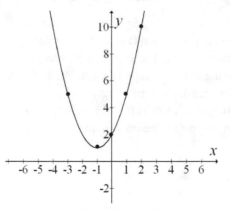

Figure 3: Plot of $f(x) = x^2 + 2x + 2$

STATISTICS

Central Tendency

Mean, median, and mode are different methods of measuring the central tendency, or the "middle," of a data set. **Mean**, or average, is the most popular measure because it can be calculated easily. **Median** is the middle point when you sort the data from lowest to highest. **Mode** is the most common or frequently occurring value in a data set. Table 2 shows the different measurements along with advantages and disadvantages.

Table 2: Central Tendency Calculations			
	Equation	**Advantages**	**Disadvantages**
Mean	$\text{avg} = \dfrac{x_1 + x_2 + \dots x_n}{n}$	• Easy to calculate • Most common method	• Influenced by outliers[1] in data
Median	Odd data points = middle value of a sequence Even data points = average of two middle points	• Good for eliminating outliers in data	• Can be inconvenient to calculate
Mode	Most frequently occurring value	• Good for well formed normal data • Good when you want to know the most common value	• Not good for sparsely populated data

Dispersion

Data is not always exact. Just knowing the mean, median, or mode of the data isn't always the full story. **Dispersion** is a measure of the spread or the deviation of the data from the central tendency. **Range** and **standard deviation** are the two most popular methods for measuring dispersion. A small range or small standard deviation means that the data are close to the mean. At times, variance is used. Standard deviation is the square root of variance. Table 3 shows the equations.

---

1 A statistical value that is outside other values in a set of data

Table 3: Measures of Dispersion

	Equation	Advantages	Disadvantages
Range	Range = highest value – lowest value	• Easy to calculate • Easily understood	• Only uses two data points • Influenced by outliers
Standard Deviation	$sd = \sqrt{\sum_{i=1}^{n} \dfrac{(x_i - \bar{x})^2}{n-1}}$ x_i = data point x = data average n = sample number	• Very popular method	• More difficult to calculate

Normal distribution is one of the most important data distributions. The data is spread symmetrically about the mean. Figure 4 shows the graph of a normal distribution. Each vertical line is one standard deviation from the mean. The mean ± 1 standard deviation represents 68 percent of the data. Said another way, 68 percent of the data will fall within ± 1 sigma. The mean ± 2 standard deviation represents 95 percent of the data. Lastly, ± 3 sigma (sometimes called 6 sigma) represents 99.7 percent of the data.

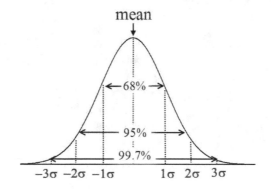

Figure 4: Normal Distribution

The **standard error** is a way of measuring the sampling fluctuation in a set of data. **Sampling fluctuation** is how much a statistic fluctuates from sample to sample. Sampling error can be calculated with the following equation:

$$SE_{\bar{x}} = \frac{\sigma}{\sqrt{n}}$$

Where:

σ = standard deviation

n = number of samples

Statistical Significance

Statistical significance is a measure of the reliability of a result or how confident you are that the outcome of an experiment happened by chance or not. In other words, did the result you obtained occur by chance, or is the result statistically significant? The level of significance is indicated by the symbol α. For example, if there is a 1-in-100 chance an event could occur, then $\alpha = 1/100$, or 0.01.

For example, if we believed one group of kids cheated on a test and another group did not, we'd look to see if the average grades of the two groups for this test were significantly different. The following measures would help us to make the decision:

1. The mean of the two groups are greater. A greater difference between the mean shows greater significant difference.
2. The measurement uncertainty or "noise" is smaller. A lower standard deviation increases significance.
3. The sample size is larger. The larger a sample size, the greater chance the data will be accurate and less susceptible to outliers.

There is always the possibility that a mistake can be made when testing for significance.

Two types of errors can occur:

1. A **Type I** error occurs when you assume that something is true when in fact it is false.
2. A **Type II** error occurs when you believe something to be false when in fact it is true.

Probability Distributions and Expected Value

When you roll dice, flip a coin, or count the number of cars that drive past your house each hour, these measures are random variables. A **random variable** is something that changes every time it is tested. The results of a random variable can be placed into groups of expected outcomes. The chance that a result falls into one of these groups or bins is its **probability**.

Example 12: Maurice believes a six-sided die isn't evenly weighted and not rolling fairly. To test his belief, he rolls the die 1,000 times. A 1 came up 150 times. A 2 was rolled 160 times. 3, 4, and 5 all came up 170 times each, and 6 came up 180 times. Create a probability table for the random variable.

Solution: The probability is calculated by dividing each roll count by the total number of rolls. The probability a 1 is rolled is 150/1,000, or 0.15. The probability for each roll is calculated and placed in the following table.

x	1	2	3	4	5	6
$P(x)$	0.15	0.16	0.17	0.17	0.17	0.18

If the random variables can take on the values $x_1, x_2, x_3, x_4 \ldots x_n$ and the probability for each outcome is $p_1, p_2, p_3, p_4, \ldots p_n$, then the expected value is

$$E(x) = x_1 p_1 + x_2 p_2 + x_3 p_3 + x_4 p_4 + \ldots + x_n p_n$$

Example 13: Using the die from Example 12, what is the expected value when you roll the die? What would be the expected value of a fair and evenly weighted six-sided die?

Solution: Use the expected value equation to solve:

$$E(x) = (0.15)(1) + (0.16)(2) + (0.17)(3) + (0.17)(4) + (0.17)(5) + (0.18)(6)$$

$$= 0.15 + 0.32 + 0.51 + 0.68 + 0.85 + 1.08$$

$$= 3.59$$

If the die were weighted evenly, then the probability of rolling any number would be the same: 1/6.

$$E(x) = \left(\frac{1}{6}\right)(1) + \left(\frac{1}{6}\right)(2) + \left(\frac{1}{6}\right)(3) + \left(\frac{1}{6}\right)(4) + \left(\frac{1}{6}\right)(5) + \left(\frac{1}{6}\right)(6)$$
$$= 3.5$$

The unevenly weighted die is more likely to roll a higher number than the evenly weighted die.

Weighted Averages

An average where each value is given a different importance or weight is the **weighted average**. If we let w_i be the weight of each value, we have the following equation:

$$\text{Weighted Average}(x) = \frac{w_1 + w_2 x_2 + \ldots + w_n x_n}{w_1 + w_2 + \ldots + w_n}$$

Example 14: Tests count for 70% of a student's grade in a senior algebra class, homework 10%, attendance 5%, and quizzes 15%. If Maria has a test average of 88, a homework average of 95, a quiz average of 95, and perfect attendance, what is her overall grade in this class?

Solution: Use the weighted average equation:

$$
\begin{aligned}
\text{Grade} &= \frac{(70)(88) + (10)(95) + (15)(95) + (5)(100)}{70 + 10 + 5 + 15} \\
&= \frac{9{,}035}{100} \\
&= 90.35
\end{aligned}
$$

Percentiles

The amount of data that falls above or below a given value is called the **percentile**. For example, 30% of the data should fall below the 30th percentile. The median is actually the 50% percentile, as there are as many values above 50% as there are below.

There is no one method for calculating percentiles. However, a widely accepted method to estimate the percentile is as follows:

1. Rank the data set by ordering the values from smallest to largest.
2. Determine the number of data points N.
3. Calculate n using the equation below where p is the percentile:

$$n = \frac{N}{100} p + \frac{1}{2}$$

4. Round this number to the nearest integer.
5. The nth value of your ranked data will be the number that represents that percentile.

BUSINESS APPLICATIONS

Index Numbers

Index numbers are used to compare data of different sizes. Index numbers show the relative changes in a variable. Index numbers are calculated just like percentages.

$$\text{Index Number} = \frac{\text{Current Value of the Indicator}}{\text{Base Period Value of the Indicator}} \times 100$$

Example 15: A house in Valley Oaks just sold for $250,000. In 2000, the same house sold for $125,000. What is the index number for the house relative to 2000?

Solution: Divide $250,000 by $125,000 multiplied by 100 for an index of 200.

Interest

Interest is the fee paid when someone uses someone else's money. You pay interest when you borrow money. The bank pays you interest to use your money when you deposit it in an account. The amount of the loan or original deposit is the principal. There are several methods used to calculate interest.

Simple interest is calculated on the principal amount; the interest is never added back into the principal. It is the most basic method for calculating return. It is a fixed, nongrowing return. The equation for simple interest is:

$$i = PVrt$$

Where:

$$PV = \text{principal or present value (\$)}$$

$$r = \text{annual interest rate (decimal)}$$

$$t = \text{number of years (in years)}$$

The future value, or maturity value, at the end of t years for simple interest FV is:

$$FV = PV(1 + rt)$$

Where:

$$i = \text{interest rate per period (decimal)}$$

$$m = \text{compounding periods per year (number)}$$

The present value P of simple interest is:

$$PV = \frac{FV}{1 + rt}$$

Compound interest adds the interest to the principal at a predetermined period. When the interest is added to the principal, the annual returns will grow every period. The present value of compound interest is:

$$PV = \frac{FV}{\left(1 + \dfrac{r}{m}\right)^{mt}}$$

The future value of compound interest is:

$$FV = PV\left(1 + \frac{r}{m}\right)^{mt}$$

Continuous interest is the answer to the question, "What happens if you compound interest at an infinitely small time frame?" The future value of continuous interest is:

$$FV = PVe^{rt}$$

Depreciation and Salvage Value

For accounting purposes, a company needs to know how much it is worth. The worth of a company is its **assets**. A company's buildings, tools, and other objects are part of its assets. Unfortunately, these assets get less valuable over time as they wear out and age. **Depreciation** is the process of putting a value to the company's changing assets.

The equation for depreciation is:

$$\text{Depreciation} = \frac{\text{Cost} - \text{Residual Value}}{\text{Estimated Useful Life}}$$

The **cost** is what the company paid for the item. The **estimated useful life** is how long the company believes the item has value. The **residual value** or salvage value is what the item is worth when it is fully depreciated.

Discounts and Credit Terms

The conditions under which the loan is given are the **credit terms**. One type of credit term is a cash discount, which is an incentive offered to purchasers of a product for payment within a specified period. The **credit period** is the amount of time to pay off the loan.

Invoices often include the credit term for when the customer must pay and define the sales discount if one was included. For example, the terms for a discount are usually written in the form of 2/15, n/30. This means that there is a 2% discount if paid in 15 days, or the net is due in 30 days.

Example 16: A man purchases $100 worth of merchandise with credit terms 5/10, n/30. If he pays in 8 days, what does he owe?

Solution: 5% of $100 is $5, which is subtracted from $100. The man owes $95.

Installment Purchases

Installment purchases are a form of credit where payments are made in installments over a fixed period, usually monthly. The lender owns the item until it is paid off, but the buyer gets to use the product.

The **amount financed** is the borrowed amount, and the **down payment** is what is paid up front:

$$\text{Amount Financed} = \text{Cash Price} - \text{Down Payment}$$

The **finance charge** is the total of the payments minus the amount financed:

$$\text{Total Finance Charge} = \text{Total of All Payments} - \text{Amount Financed}$$

The deferred payment price is what the item really costs:

$$\text{Deferred Payment Price} = \text{Total of All Payments} + \text{Down Payment}$$

The monthly payment can be calculated using the formula:

$$\text{Monthly Payment} = \frac{\text{Finance Charge} + \text{Amount Financed}}{\text{Number of Payments}}$$

Markup and Markdown

The selling price for an item is not the cost the seller paid for it. For the seller to make money, the seller needs to add markup to the price of the item. **Markup** allows the seller to make a profit on his sale as well as pay for labor costs, property rental, taxes, and other expenses that are required to operate the business.

$$\text{Selling Price} = \text{Cost} + \text{Markup}$$

or:

$$\text{Selling Price} = \text{Cost}(1 + \% \text{ Markup})$$

Markdown is the amount a seller discounts a product to encourage sales:

$$\text{Markdown \%} = \frac{\text{Dollar Markdown}}{\text{Original Selling Price}} \times 100$$

Taxes

Governments use taxes to raise revenue. **Sales taxes** are usually added as a percentage of the sale price. Other taxes include **excise tax**, which is a fixed or percentage tax placed on luxury and nonessential items such as tobacco.

Property tax is a tax placed on the value of property. The value the government (through the local county assessor's office) assigns to a property is its **assessed value**. Generally, the amount of property tax is based on a tax rate. The tax rate is often based on budget needs:

$$\text{Tax Rate} = \frac{\text{Budget Needed}}{\text{Total Assessed Value}}$$

The amount of property tax paid is:

$$\text{Property Tax} = \text{Tax Rate} \times \text{Total Assessed Value}$$

Cost Calculations

There are two types of costs—**fixed costs** and **variable costs**. Fixed costs are expenses that do not increase or decrease with the number of products produced. On the other hand, variable costs increase with the number of units produced. Total cost is the sum of fixed and variable costs.

$C(x)$ represents the total cost of manufacturing x number of items, m represents the cost per unit or marginal cost, and F represents the total fixed costs:

$$C(x) = mx + F$$

Example 17: If the total cost for manufacturing watches is $C(x) = 3x + 500$, what would the fixed costs be? What would be the cost of manufacturing 1,000 watches?

Solution: For fixed cost, let $x = 0$ and solve for $C(x)$:

$$C(0) = 3(0) + 500$$

$$= 500$$

Fixed cost = \$500. For 1,000 watches, let $x = 1,000$ and solve:

$$C(1,000) = 3(1,000) + 500$$

$$= 3,500$$

Total cost = \$3,500

The average cost to manufacture is the total cost divided by the number of units manufactured. For example, the average cost of watches for 1,000 watches manufactured would be 3,500/1,000, or \$3.50 per watch.

Break-even Analysis

Break-even is the point where the revenue generated by a product will equal the cost of manufacturing. After the break-even point, a product can produce a profit. Like cost, we can plot revenue where $R(x) = px$, with p being the marginal revenue, or how much money is made per item. **Profit** is the revenue minus the cost:

$$\text{Profit} = \text{Revenue} - \text{Cost}$$

Example 18: Graph the break-even point if the fixed cost to manufacture a toothbrush is $10,000, and the marginal cost is $2 per item. The toothbrush can be sold for $4 per item. Next, find the break-even point without graphing. What would the profit be if 20,000 items were sold?

Solution: Plot the two lines and find the intersect point. $C(x) = 2x + 10,000$ and $R(x) = 4x$:

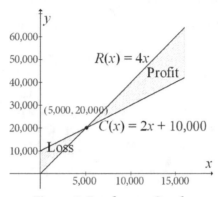

Figure 5: Break-even Graph

You can see that the break-even point occurs at the manufacturing of 5,000 units. To find the solution without graphing, we need to set the two equations equal to each other:

$$C(x) = R(x)$$
$$2x + 10,000 = 4x$$
$$2x = 10,000$$
$$x = 5,000$$

Again, we arrive at the solution of 5,000 units to break even. Next, find the profit if 15,000 units are sold:

$$P(x) = R(x) - C(x)$$
$$P(20,000) = 4(20,000) - (2(20,000) + 10,000)$$
$$= 80,000 - 40,000 - 10,000$$
$$x = 30,000$$

The profit for selling 20,000 units would be $30,000.

Financial Ratio Calculation and Analysis

The relationship of one number to another can be expressed with a **ratio**. Companies use ratios to compare various measures from one year to another to spot trends. Ratios can be used to compare one company to another.

Here are some examples of common financial ratios.

Current Ratio—The current ratio is the best measure of financial strength:

$$\text{Current Ratio} = \frac{\text{Total Current Assets}}{\text{Total Current Liabilities}}$$

The main question answered by the current ratio is, "Does the business have enough current assets to meet the payment schedule of its current debts?" A healthy ratio is 2 to 1. A ratio below 1 to 1 means that there are not enough assets compared to debts.

Quick Ratio—The quick ratio or "acid-test" ratio is the best measure of liquidity:

$$\text{Quick Ratio} = \frac{\text{Cash} + \text{Government Securities} + \text{Receivables}}{\text{Total Current Liabilities}}$$

The quick ratio excludes inventories in the assets and focuses on liquid assets. It answers the question, "If sales revenues dropped to zero, could the business pay its current debt?" A 1:1 ratio is considered good.

Leverage Ratio—The leverage ratio measures how much a business is using debt financing as opposed to their equity:

$$\text{Leverage Ratio} = \frac{\text{Total Liabilities}}{\text{Net Worth}}$$

The leverage ratio answers the question, "How much does this business rely on credit?" The higher this ratio, the more trouble this business could be in if credit becomes difficult to obtain.

Many other ratios exist. You can find these ratios in finance books or on the Internet.

Trend analysis uses ratios to uncover changes from year to year. A base year is required for each metric. Each individual value is then divided by the base value. Trend analysis is a form of normalization expressed as a percentage. See the example below of how to use trend analysis for sales from year to year.

Example 19: Use trend analysis to compare the sales from various years using 2015 as the base year. 2014 = $20,000; 2015 = $22,000; 2016 = $25,000; 2017 = $18,000.

Solution: Divide each year's sales by $22,000.

Year:	2014	2015	2016	2017
Sales:	$= \dfrac{20,000}{22,000}$ $= 91\%$	$= \dfrac{22,000}{22,000}$ $= 100\%$	$= \dfrac{25,000}{22,000}$ $= 114\%$	$= \dfrac{18,000}{22,000}$ $= 82\%$

Promissory Notes and Other Loans

The **promissory note** is a contract between a borrower and a lender that puts loan information in writing. Many lenders require a signed promissory note from a borrower when lending money. The note states that the borrower will repay the money at a fixed interval. The note can be interest bearing or noninterest bearing, depending on whether interest is included or not. The note will include the names of the parties, the amount of the loan, the interest rate if any, and the payment schedule. Other information may be included as well. A promissory note differs from an IOU, which states only that a debt exists.

A loan that is repaid at one time is called a **single payment**. With **amortized payments**, the borrower pays a set amount each period, usually a month or a year, until the loan is paid in full. A **balloon payment** requires periodic payments of principal and interest for a set amount of time. After the last payment, the remaining principal and interest are owed in one large payment. Another type of balloon payment is the **interest-only balloon payment**. With this type of balloon payment, the borrower pays the lender regular payments of only the interest and then one final balloon payment of all of the principal and remaining interest.

Interpretation of Graphical Representations

Graphs are a valuable method for giving data meaning. With computers, it's very easy to create nice-looking graphs, but it's also very easy to create inaccurate or ineffective graphs. It's important to choose the right type of graph and use it in the correct way. If a graph doesn't clearly convey the meaning of the numbers, then it is not serving its purpose.

There are many types of graphs:

- *Bar graph*: bars compare a single set of statistics for different categories of data.
- *Line Graph*: lines connect data points to show changes over time.
- *Histogram*: bars represent the frequency of numerical data ranges.
- *Scatter Plot*: two variables are plotted against each other usually without lines.
- *Pie Chart*: a circle is sliced into pieces that represent parts of the whole.

Here are a few rules for making a graph:

1. The graph should have a title that clearly states what the graph is illustrating.
2. The *x*-axis should be the independent variable, and the *y*-axis the dependent variable.
3. Axes should be labeled and numbered.
4. A key should identify each line type.
5. Fancy 3-D effects should be avoided, and pie charts used as infrequently as possible.

Graphs can be used to misrepresent information. For example, numbers can be left off the axes to avoid clearly showing what is happening with the data. The *y*-axis might not begin with a zero value, and changes might be exaggerated by not showing a full scale on the *y*-axis. Fancy 3-D effects can also be used to hide data in the background or to distort the relative size of the data. As a rule of thumb, pie charts should rarely be used. Often the size of the pie slice is difficult to compare, especially when the percentages are not included.

Interpolation and Extrapolation

When dealing with line graphs and scatter plots, you may want to predict values that are not represented in the existing data set. A **regression line**, a line that best fits the trend of the given data, can be used to predict these values by plugging an x value into the line $y = mx + b$ and finding the corresponding y value. If the x for which you are finding y is within the range of the original data, the prediction is called **interpolation**.

NOTE: Linear equations are equations of a straight line. They are usually presented in the form $y = mx + b$, where m is the slope, and b is the point where the line intercepts the *y*-axis. Linear interpolation results in a straight line. Curved interpolation is used when dealing with polynomial and other advanced equations.

When you need to construct new data points outside of your known data points, you can use extrapolation. Extrapolation is a way to make a "best guess" or estimate, based on the trend of the existing data, about the future or a hypothetical situation. An assumption exists with extrapolation that the linear relationship will remain valid outside of the original data range. This assumption may or may not be justified, depending upon the specific situation.

For example, if a vendor sells 40 cups of hot cocoa when it is 30° F, and 80 cups when it is 25°F, he could predict that he will sell 160 cups of hot cocoa when the temperature hits 20°. But there's no way to be certain that will be the case.

As with interpolation, there are various extrapolation methods available to achieve linear or curved projections. However, because its results are more uncertain, extrapolation is less reliable than interpolation and should be used with care.

Unit Conversions

It is often necessary to convert units when working with data. Changing inches to centimeters is a common conversion. Changing one currency to another requires some knowledge in converting units.

The best method for converting units is to set up the conversion in a table as shown below. Do not take shortcuts when doing a conversion, no matter how simple a conversion may seem.

In the table below, dollars per hour are being converted to yen per day. Notice that units are kept with the numbers and canceled. The use of this type of table helps you keep up with the units and make certain you are multiplying and dividing by the correct amounts.

$$\frac{5 \text{ dollars}}{\text{hour}} \left| \frac{95 \text{ yen}}{1 \text{ dollar}} \right| \frac{24 \text{ hours}}{1 \text{ day}} = \frac{(5)(95)(24) \text{ yen}}{\text{day}} = 11,400 \text{ yen per day}$$

Investment Performance Measures

The **P/E ratio**, or **price-to-earnings ratio**, is the measure of a company's current share price compared to its per-share earnings. For example, if a company is trading at $20 a share and the earnings for the last year were $2 per share, the P/E ratio would be 10.0. The higher the P/E ratio, the more demand there is for a stock. The P/E ratio's unit is in years, as it refers to the number of years it will take to pay back the stock purchase price.

$$P/E\ Ratio = \frac{Price\ per\ Share}{Annual\ Earnings\ per\ Share}$$

The **rate of return (ROR)** is a measure of the money gained or lost on an investment relative to the money invested. It is also known as return on investment, or ROI. The single-period arithmetic return is:

$$Rate\ of\ Return = \frac{Final\ Value\ -\ Initial\ Value}{Initial\ Value}$$

Stock yield, or current dividend yield, percentage tells stockholders what the dividend per share is returning:

$$Stock\ Yield = \frac{Annual\ Dividend\ per\ Share}{Current\ Share\ Price}$$

Cost Minimization and Value Optimization

In the discussion of the break-even point, it is clear that the higher the price you receive for a product, the fewer units you need to produce to break even. However, the higher the price, the fewer units you will sell and the longer it will take to break even. So how do you set a price?

Obviously, to make a profit, the selling price must be above the cost of the unit. The lower the cost of the unit, the more money can be made when it is sold. For many products with stiff price competition, finding ways to lower costs is the only way to make a profit and survive in the market place.

The product's value is what the customer thinks the product or service is worth. The more the customer thinks the product is worth, the more the customer is willing to pay. The value of a product can be increased any number of ways. Advertising makes a product more desirable in the eye of the consumer. Improving quality or adding additional features can also increase value by distinguishing a product from a competitor's product.

FINANCIAL MATHEMATICS

Annuities—Present and Future Value

An **annuity** is a stream of fixed payments or receipts made over a specified period. An ordinary annuity is one where the payment is made at the end of the payment period. The equation for calculating the present value of an ordinary annuity, where PMT is the periodic payment, is:

$$PV_{OA} = PMT \left[\frac{1 - \dfrac{1}{\left(1 + \dfrac{r}{m}\right)^{tm}}}{\dfrac{r}{m}} \right]$$

The annuity can be calculated based on the present value of the loan:

$$PMT_{OA} = PV \left[\frac{\dfrac{r}{m}}{\left(1 + \dfrac{r}{m}\right)^{mn} - 1} \right] \left(1 + \frac{r}{m}\right)^{mn}$$

The future value of an ordinary annuity can be calculated:

$$FV_{OA} = PMT \left[\frac{\left(1 + \dfrac{r}{m}\right)^{mn} - 1}{\dfrac{r}{m}} \right]$$

With an annuity due, the payment is made at the beginning of the payment period. The equation for the present value of an annuity due is:

$$PV_{AD} = PMT \left[\frac{1 - \dfrac{1}{\left(1 + \dfrac{r}{m}\right)^{tm}}}{\dfrac{r}{m}} \right] \left(1 + \frac{r}{m}\right)$$

Where:

PV_{OA} = present value of an ordinary annuity

PMT_{OA} = amount of each payment

PV_{AD} = present value of an ordinary annuity

r = yearly nominal interest rate (in decimal, or % ÷ 100)

t = number of years

m = number of periods per year

PMT = periodic payment

....

IMPORTANT NOTE: $\frac{r}{m}$ replaces i, the annual interest, in the equations in this section, so that you will clearly understand what interest is used in the calculation.

....

The future value of an ordinary annuity is the value of expected periodic payments after a period of time:

$$FV_{OA} = PMT \left[\frac{\left(1 + \frac{r}{m}\right)^{mn} - 1}{\frac{r}{m}} \right]$$

The future value can be calculated for an annuity due:

$$FV_{AD} = PMT \left[\frac{\left(1 + \frac{r}{m}\right)^{tm} - 1}{\frac{r}{m}} \right] \left(1 + \frac{r}{m}\right)$$

Amortization

A loan is **amortized** if the principal and interest are paid by a sequence of equal periodic payments. It is a process of reducing the balance of a loan by a periodic payment. The following equation can be used to calculate the payment for an amortization loan made at the end of each period:

$$PMT_{Amort} = \frac{PV\left(\frac{r}{m}\right)}{1 - \left(1 + \frac{r}{m}\right)^{-mt}}$$

Banks use amortization tables because they require exact calculations; however, the remaining balance of an amortization can be approximated by the following equation:

$$y_{Amort} = PMT \left[\frac{1 - \left(1 + \dfrac{r}{m}\right)^{-(mt-x)}}{\dfrac{r}{m}} \right]$$

Where:

$$x = \text{number of payments made}$$

You can calculate the amount of the total interest paid on a loan with the following calculation:

Amount Paid in Interest = Total Payments Made – Amount of the Loan

Annual Percentage Rate

The **annual percentage rate** (**APR**) is a term created to help convey what the annual cost of the loan will be in a percentage. Nominal APR is a simple-interest rate for a year. Effective APR, or EAR, includes fees such as participation fees, loan origination fees, monthly service fees, or late charges. The effective APR is the true annual interest rate paid when it is all said and done.

Effective Annual Rate

The **effective rate** is the actual rate that you earn on an investment or pay on a loan when interest is compounded more than once a year. The effective interest rate does not incorporate one-time charges or front-end fees. The effective rate of an investment will always be higher than the nominal or stated interest rate. The equation for effective rate of compounded interest r_E is:

$$r_E = \left(1 + \frac{r}{m}\right)^m - 1$$

The effective rate for continuous interest is:

$$r_E = e^r - 1$$

Note: With these types of problems, you will be working with numbers raised to very large powers. It is not uncommon for hand calculators, spreadsheets, or calculators from websites to be off by a few cents.

SUMMING IT UP

- There are three common ways to use numbers to describe a part of a whole: **fractions**, **decimals**, and **percentages**. Percentage means "per cent" or "out of 100."
- **Linear equations** are equations of a straight line and usually appear as $y = mx + b$, where m is the slope and b is the point where the line intercepts the y-axis.
- An **inequality** is a math statement that, instead of an equal sign, uses one of the following symbols: "greater than" ($>$), "less than" ($<$), "greater than or equal to" ($\geq$), or "less than or equal to" ($\leq$).
- Equations having more than one variable are **simultaneous equations**. The substitution method is the easiest way to solve simultaneous equations.
- A **quadratic equation** contains a variable of the second order, for example, $3x^2 - 2x + 5$. Solve quadratic equations by finding where the equation equals zero.
- Evaluating a function requires finding the values that are true for the function. Graphing the points helps you know what the function looks like.
- **Mean**, **median**, and **mode** are methods of measuring the central tendency, or the "middle," of a data set.
- **Dispersion** is a measure of the spread or the deviation of the data from the central tendency. **Range** and **standard deviation** are two methods for measuring dispersion. A small range or small standard deviation means that the data are close to the mean.
- **Statistical significance** is a measure of the reliability of a result. The level of significance is indicated by the symbol α. **Type I** errors occur when one assumes that something is true when it is false; **Type II** errors occur when one believes something to be false when it is true.
- The **standard error** is a way of measuring the sampling fluctuation in a set of data. **Sampling fluctuation** is how much a statistic fluctuates from sample to sample.
- A **random variable** is something that changes every time it is tested. The results of a random variable can be placed into groups of expected outcomes. The chance that a result falls into one of these groups or bins is its **probability**.
- An average where each value is given a different importance or weight is the **weighted average**.
- A **percentile** is the amount of data that falls above or below a given value. For example, 30% of the data falls below the 30th percentile. The median is the 50% percentile, as there are as many values above 50% as there are below.

- **Index numbers** are used to compare data of different sizes.
- **Interest** is the fee paid when someone uses someone else's money. **Principal** is the amount of the loan or original deposit. **Simple interest** is calculated on the principal amount; the interest is never added back into the principal. **Compound interest** adds the interest to the principal at a predetermined period.
- **Depreciation** is the process of putting a value to a company's changing assets. The cost is what the company paid for the item, the estimated useful life is how long the company believes the item has value, and the residual or salvage value is what the item is worth when fully depreciated.
- A **cash discount** is an incentive offered to purchasers of a product for payment within a specified period. The **credit period** is the amount of time to pay off the loan. The terms for a discount are usually written in the form of 2/15, *n*/30. This means that there is a 2% discount if paid in 15 days, or the net is due in 30 days.
- **Installment purchases** are a form of credit where payments are made in parts over a fixed period of time. Until it is paid off, the lender owns the item, but the buyer can use it. The **borrowed amount** is the amount financed. The down payment is what is paid up front. The **finance charge** is the total of the payments minus the amount financed. The **deferred payment** price is what the item really costs.
- **Markup** allows the seller to make a profit on his sale as well as pay for labor costs, property rental, taxes, and other expenses that are required to operate the business. **Markdown** is the amount a seller discounts a product to encourage sales.
- **Sales tax** is usually added as a percentage of the sale price. **Excise tax** is a fixed or percentage tax placed on luxury and nonessential items. **Property tax** is a tax placed on the value of property. The value the government assigns to a property is its **assessed value**.
- **Break-even** is the point where the revenue generated by a product equals the cost of manufacturing. After the break-even point, a product can produce a profit. **Profit** is the revenue minus the cost.
- **Ratios** are used by companies to compare various measures from one year to another to spot trends. Common financial ratios include current ratio, quick or "acid test" ratio, and leverage ratio. Trend analysis ratios uncover changes from year to year and are expressed as percentages.
- The **promissory note** is a contract between a borrower and a lender that puts loan information in writing.
- A **single payment loan** is repaid at one time. With **amortized payments**, you pay a set amount each period until the loan is paid in full. A **balloon**

payment requires periodic payments of principal and interest for a set amount of time, and after the last payment, the remaining principal and interest are owed in one large payment.

- Graphs are a valuable method for giving data meaning, but it must clearly convey the meaning of the numbers. Types of graphs include **bar graphs**, **histograms**, **line graphs**, **scatter plots**, and **pie charts**.

- **Interpolation** is a method of fitting a line or other data points between two known points. Linear interpolation draws a straight line. Curved interpolation uses polynomial and other advanced equations. **Extrapolation** creates data based on the trend of known data; it is less reliable than interpolation.

- The **P/E (price-to-earnings)** ratio is the measure of a company's current share price compared to its per-share earnings. The **rate of return (ROR)** or **return on investment (ROI)** is a measure of the money gained or lost on an investment relative to the money invested. **Stock yield**, or current dividend yield, percentage tells stockholders what the dividend per share is returning.

- To make a **profit**, the selling price must be above the cost of the unit. The lower the cost of the unit, the more money can be made when it is sold. The product's value is what the customer thinks the product or service is worth.

- An **annuity** is a stream of fixed payments or receipts made over a specified period. An ordinary annuity is one where the payment is made at the end of the payment period. The future value of an ordinary annuity is the value of expected periodic payments after a period of time.

- A loan is **amortized** if the principal and interest are paid by a sequence of equal periodic payments. It is a process of reducing the balance of a loan by a periodic payment. Amount paid in interest = total payments made – amount of the loan.

- The **annual percentage rate (APR)** conveys what the annual cost of the loan will be in a percentage. **Nominal APR** is a simple-interest rate for a year. **Effective APR (EAR)** includes participation fees, loan origination fees, monthly service fees, or late charges and is the true annual interest rate paid.

Chapter 4

Business Mathematics Post-Test

POST-TEST ANSWER SHEET

1. Ⓐ Ⓑ Ⓒ Ⓓ

2. Ⓐ Ⓑ Ⓒ Ⓓ

3. Ⓐ Ⓑ Ⓒ Ⓓ

4. Ⓐ Ⓑ Ⓒ Ⓓ

5. Ⓐ Ⓑ Ⓒ Ⓓ

6. Ⓐ Ⓑ Ⓒ Ⓓ

7. Ⓐ Ⓑ Ⓒ Ⓓ

8. Ⓐ Ⓑ Ⓒ Ⓓ

9. Ⓐ Ⓑ Ⓒ Ⓓ

10. Ⓐ Ⓑ Ⓒ Ⓓ

11. Ⓐ Ⓑ Ⓒ Ⓓ

12. Ⓐ Ⓑ Ⓒ Ⓓ

13. Ⓐ Ⓑ Ⓒ Ⓓ

14. Ⓐ Ⓑ Ⓒ Ⓓ

15. Ⓐ Ⓑ Ⓒ Ⓓ

16. Ⓐ Ⓑ Ⓒ Ⓓ

17. Ⓐ Ⓑ Ⓒ Ⓓ

18. Ⓐ Ⓑ Ⓒ Ⓓ

19. Ⓐ Ⓑ Ⓒ Ⓓ

20. Ⓐ Ⓑ Ⓒ Ⓓ

21. Ⓐ Ⓑ Ⓒ Ⓓ

22. Ⓐ Ⓑ Ⓒ Ⓓ

23. Ⓐ Ⓑ Ⓒ Ⓓ

24. Ⓐ Ⓑ Ⓒ Ⓓ

25. Ⓐ Ⓑ Ⓒ Ⓓ

26. Ⓐ Ⓑ Ⓒ Ⓓ

27. Ⓐ Ⓑ Ⓒ Ⓓ

28. Ⓐ Ⓑ Ⓒ Ⓓ

29. Ⓐ Ⓑ Ⓒ Ⓓ

30. Ⓐ Ⓑ Ⓒ Ⓓ

31. Ⓐ Ⓑ Ⓒ Ⓓ

32. Ⓐ Ⓑ Ⓒ Ⓓ

33. Ⓐ Ⓑ Ⓒ Ⓓ

34. Ⓐ Ⓑ Ⓒ Ⓓ

35. Ⓐ Ⓑ Ⓒ Ⓓ

36. Ⓐ Ⓑ Ⓒ Ⓓ

37. Ⓐ Ⓑ Ⓒ Ⓓ

38. Ⓐ Ⓑ Ⓒ Ⓓ

39. Ⓐ Ⓑ Ⓒ Ⓓ

40. Ⓐ Ⓑ Ⓒ Ⓓ

41. Ⓐ Ⓑ Ⓒ Ⓓ

42. Ⓐ Ⓑ Ⓒ Ⓓ

43. Ⓐ Ⓑ Ⓒ Ⓓ

44. Ⓐ Ⓑ Ⓒ Ⓓ

45. Ⓐ Ⓑ Ⓒ Ⓓ

46. Ⓐ Ⓑ Ⓒ Ⓓ

47. Ⓐ Ⓑ Ⓒ Ⓓ

48. Ⓐ Ⓑ Ⓒ Ⓓ

49. Ⓐ Ⓑ Ⓒ Ⓓ   **53.** Ⓐ Ⓑ Ⓒ Ⓓ   **57.** Ⓐ Ⓑ Ⓒ Ⓓ

50. Ⓐ Ⓑ Ⓒ Ⓓ   **54.** Ⓐ Ⓑ Ⓒ Ⓓ   **58.** Ⓐ Ⓑ Ⓒ Ⓓ

51. Ⓐ Ⓑ Ⓒ Ⓓ   **55.** Ⓐ Ⓑ Ⓒ Ⓓ   **59.** Ⓐ Ⓑ Ⓒ Ⓓ

52. Ⓐ Ⓑ Ⓒ Ⓓ   **56.** Ⓐ Ⓑ Ⓒ Ⓓ   **60.** Ⓐ Ⓑ Ⓒ Ⓓ

BUSINESS MATHEMATICS POST-TEST

Directions: Carefully read each of the following 60 questions. Choose the best answer to each question and fill in the corresponding circle on the answer sheet. The Answer Key and Explanations can be found following this post-test.

1. If Leon ate one third of an apple pie, one fourth of a cherry pie, and one fourth of a pecan pie, how much total pie did Leon eat?

   A. $\frac{1}{6}$

   B. $\frac{3}{11}$

   C. $\frac{5}{12}$

   D. $\frac{5}{6}$

2. A concrete mixer is purchased from a hardware store on installments. Who legally owns the concrete mixer if the second payment is missed by the buyer?

   A. The buyer
   B. The hardware store
   C. The bank
   D. None of the above

3. What is an amortized loan?

   A. A loan where only interest is paid
   B. A loan repaid in a one-time payment of both interest and principal
   C. A loan where payments are made each period to pay off interest and principal
   D. None of the above

4. What is the effective annual interest rate for a continuously compounded interest rate of 12%?

   A. 1.0%
   B. 12.0%
   C. 12.68%
   D. 12.75%

5. Which of the following defines P/E ratio?

   A. Performance-to-equity ratio
   B. Price-to-earnings ratio
   C. Profit-to-expense ratio
   D. Principal-to-equity ratio

6. Crystal is looking at credit cards and notices that the APR on her credit card is 19.2%. What is the monthly interest rate?

   A. 1.6%
   B. 1.75%
   C. 20.98%
   D. 21.17%

7. Solve the equation $3x^2 - 3x + \dfrac{1}{2} = 0$.

   A. $x = -\dfrac{1}{2} \pm \dfrac{\sqrt{3}}{2}$

   B. $x = -\dfrac{1}{6} \pm \dfrac{\sqrt{3}}{6}$

   C. $x = \dfrac{1}{2} \pm \dfrac{\sqrt{3}}{2}$

   D. $x = \dfrac{1}{2} \pm \dfrac{\sqrt{3}}{6}$

8. What is wrong with the graph below?

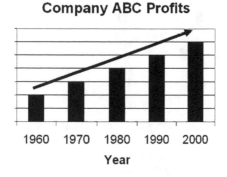

Company ABC Profits

Year

A. The arrow is distracting from the true data trend.
B. The data would be better represented with a line chart.
C. The *y*-axis label and values are missing.
D. There is nothing wrong with the graph.

9. What would be the best linear extrapolation of the points (0, 1) and (1, 3)?

A. (3, 6)
B. (–1, –1)
C. (2, 6)
D. (–3, –3)

10. A boy is in the 75th percentile for his height at his current age. What do we know about the boy?

A. He is 75% shorter than he should be for his age.
B. He will grow another 25%.
C. He is taller than 75% of the boys his age.
D. He is 75% shorter than other boys his age.

11. Which of the following functions best represents the plot in the graph below?

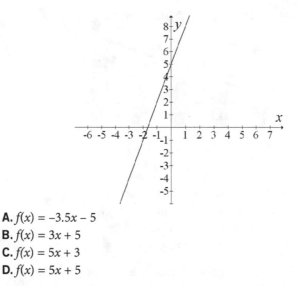

A. $f(x) = -3.5x - 5$
B. $f(x) = 3x + 5$
C. $f(x) = 5x + 3$
D. $f(x) = 5x + 5$

12. What is the difference between the mean and median for the following data points?

$$(4, 3, 6, 3, 7, 4, 5, 9, 4)$$

A. 0
B. 1
C. 2
D. 3

13. How would the credit terms be notated for a 2% discount in 20 days and net due in 30 days?

A. $20/2, 30/n$
B. $2-20/n-30$
C. $2/20, n/30$
D. $1 + n/3$

14. What is a promissory note?

A. An IOU
B. A contract between a borrower and a lender
C. A coupon promising a discount
D. All of the above

15. Dariya works at a carnival at a booth where children throw darts at balloons to win a prize. The children toss a dart until they successfully pop a balloon. When popped, each balloon reveals a prize number 1 through 4, where 4 is the most expensive prize and 1 is the least expensive. Dariya needs to prepare 100 balloons so the expected outcome if the balloons are popped at random is 1.5. She is told that there must be one #4 prize and ten #3 prizes. How many of each balloon must she prepare from 1 to 4?

    A. 70, 19, 10, 1
    B. 50, 39, 10, 1
    C. 62, 27, 10, 1
    D. 60, 29, 10, 1

16. Bryan wishes to prepare for his future retirement in 10 years. He deposits $85,000 at the end of each year for 10 years into an account paying 8% annually. How much will be in his account at the end of the 10 years?

    A. $850,450.12
    B. $1,004,565.34
    C. $1,231,357.81
    D. $1,321,577.14

17. What is the percent chance that three coins when flipped will all turn up heads?

    A. 8 percent
    B. 12.5 percent
    C. 25 percent
    D. 33 percent

18. A piano in the music store wasn't selling at $9,500, so the shop owner decided to mark it down to $6,950. What would be the markdown percentage for the piano?

    A. 20%
    B. 25%
    C. 27%
    D. 30%

19. A manufacturer estimates that he will sell 10,000 widgets. He knows that with only minor changes to his current tool set in his plant he can make widgets at $4 per unit, with a fixed cost of $9,800. How much additional fixed cost could the manufacturer spend on top of the $9,800, if the extra fixed costs achieved a variable cost of $3.50 per unit?

   A. $5,000
   B. $5,500
   C. $6,000
   D. $6,500

20. The percentage markup on a dress is 85%, and the dress is priced to sell at $185. What is the cost of the dress?

   A. $45.94
   B. $85
   C. $100
   D. $157.25

21. If a company's current ratio is 2:1, what do you know about the company?

   A. Its total current assets are half the total current liabilities.
   B. The total liabilities are twice the net worth.
   C. There are enough assets compared to debts.
   D. Total cash, securities, and receivables are twice the current liabilities.

22. Elias searched the internet for basketball prices and was amazed at how many different prices he found. He found the following prices: $19.17, $22.50, $12.95, $16.99, $17.50, $18.25, $16.99. What is the 50th percentile for these prices?

   A. $12.95
   B. $16.99
   C. $17.50
   D. $17.76

23. The index number for stock XYZ in 2000 was 250 relative to the price in 1970. If the stock was $12 per share in 1970, what was the price in 2000?

   A. $12
   B. $15
   C. $24
   D. $30

24. A company buys a dump truck for $100,000, and its salvage value is $20,000. If the company depreciates the truck over 8 years, what is its depreciation?

   A. $8,000
   B. $10,000
   C. $12,000
   D. $20,000

25. Solve the linear equations:

$$\begin{cases} 2x + y = 5 \\ 5x + 5y = 5 \end{cases}$$

   A. (2, 3)
   B. (4, –3)
   C. (2, 1)
   D. (5, –5)

26. The credit terms for a $1,000 purchase are written 3/10, $n/20$. If the customer pays in 8 days, what will the customer pay?

   A. $30
   B. $970
   C. $990
   D. $1,000

27. The total assessed value of property in the city of Cape Water-town is 32.5 million dollars. If the tax rate was 0.0648 per dollar, how much revenue will the city raise through property tax?

   A. $2,106,000
   B. $2,215,450
   C. $2,420,655
   D. $3,250,000

28. Who sets the assessed value for property?

    A. The market

    B. The property owner

    C. The owner of the property's mineral rights

    D. The government

29. If the total manufacturing cost for widgets is $C(x) = 0.17x + 50,000$, what is the cost of manufacturing 1,500 widgets?

    A. $255

    B. $49,745

    C. $50,255

    D. $75,500

30. Solve $x^2 - 6x + 5 = 0$.

    A. $(1, -0.833)$

    B. $(-1, -5)$

    C. $(5, 1)$

    D. $(1, -1.2)$

31. What would be the fixed cost to manufacture dolls if the cost per unit was $1.45 and 10,000 dolls cost $16,200?

    A. $1,450

    B. $1,620

    C. $1,650

    D. $1,700

32. If the cost for a product is $C(x) = 1.2x + 1,274$ and the product is sold for $R(x) = 6x$, how many units will need to be sold in order to break even?

    A. 263

    B. 264

    C. 265

    D. 266

33. If the standard error is 2 for a set of data where the mean is 250 and the standard deviation is 20, what is the number of data points?

    A. 40
    B. 100
    C. 250
    D. 500

34. Given the graph below, what is the number of units needed to break even, and what is the profit/cost for that number of units?

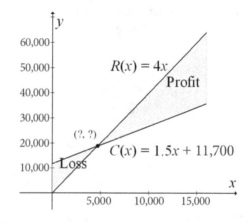

    A. 4,680; $18,720
    B. 4,000; $11,700
    C. 4,680; $11,700
    D. 4,000; $11,700

35. The following chart shows Company A's expenses from year to year. If the trend analysis is based on 2017, when expenses were $243,000, what were the expenses for 2014?

Year	2014	2015	2016	2017	2018
Expenses	85%	90%	95%	100%	72%

    A. $36,450
    B. $201,250
    C. $206,550
    D. $285,882

36. Solve the linear equation $3x - 10 = 23$.

  A. 3
  B. 4.33
  C. 9
  D. 11

37. Examine the pie chart below. If the average budget of the people represented in this graph is $3,000 per month, how much does the average person spend on food per month?

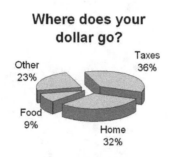

Where does your dollar go?

  A. $270
  B. $300
  C. $333
  D. The pie chart does not contain enough information to solve.

38. Given the following spreadsheet, what would be the best linear interpolated value for the unknown cell x?

1	45
7	x
15	89

  A. 53.45
  B. 62
  C. 63.86
  D. 67

39. A businesswoman spent 2,940 euros during a one-week business trip in Sicily. What were her expenses in US dollars per day if 1 euro = 1.42 US dollars?

A. $207.04
B. $295.77
C. $420
D. $596.40

40. A researcher presented a paper at a conference that showed that El Niño was responsible for increased onion production in New Mexico. However, after the paper was published, numerous other researchers showed that there was no significant difference in his data. The researcher gave a retraction at a later conference. What type of error was this?

A. Type I
B. Type II
C. Both Type I and Type II
D. It was not an error.

41. The temperature outside is 18° Celsius, where C is Celsius and F is Fahrenheit and the conversion equation is: $C = \dfrac{5}{9}(F - 32)$. What is the temperature in Fahrenheit?

A. 64.3°
B. 66.8°
C. 68.3°
D. 72.0°

42. Milo's final grades for the semester are shown in the table below. An A = 4 points, a B = 3 points, and a C = 2 points. What would be Milo's grade point average if the classes are weighted against their credit hours?

Class	Credit hours	Grade
English	3	A
Algebra	3	B
Physics	4	B
Chemistry	4	C
Phys. Ed.	2	A

A. 2.75
B. 2.85
C. 3.06
D. 3.20

43. What is the stock yield if a stock's closing price is $45 and its annual dividend per share is $2?

A. 4.4%
B. 8.8%
C. 22.5%
D. 44%

44. What is a sure way to decrease the time it takes to sell enough units to break even?

A. Lower the cost to manufacture
B. Increase the sale price
C. Lower the sale price
D. None of the above

45. What is the future value of $1,800 compounded monthly at 9.5% interest for 8 years?

A. $3,543.37
B. $3,845.40
C. $3,837.41
D. $4,225.98

46. A woman wishes to give $50 at the end of each month to a charity for two years. The interest rate that can be earned on the money is 12%. What is the present value of this gift?

A. $1,054.20
B. $1,062.17
C. $1,200
D. $1,450.69

47. Before a professor handed out the grades on the last exam, he wrote on the board that the class average was 78 with a standard deviation of 7. He also noted that the distribution of the grades was normal. Based on this information, which of the following statements is most likely true?

A. No more than 68% of the students scored between a 71 and 85.
B. No more than 34% of the students scored above a 78.
C. No more than 95% of the students' scores are between 57 and 99.
D. No one could have scored a 100.

48. A car costs $20,000. Francis will pay a $5,000 down payment and then monthly payments for three years with an interest of 10%. What is the amount of each payment?

A. $430.09
B. $445.22
C. $484.01
D. $501.25

49. If the depreciation of a $20,000 widget is $2,000 and it depreciates over 7 years, what is its salvage value?

A. $2,000
B. $3,000
C. $6,000
D. $14,000

50. What interest would be earned if $500 were invested for 5 years at 8% simple interest?

A. $200
B. $225.65
C. $250.26
D. $500

51. A family buys a house for $265,000 with a down payment of $25,000. The family takes out a 15-year mortgage at an interest rate of 5.5%. Find the amount of the monthly payment required to amortize this loan.

A. $1,362.69
B. $1,961
C. $2,117.34
D. $2,251.67

52. If Susie buys a blanket from an infomercial on TV and pays 3 easy payments of $19.95 along with a one-time down payment to upgrade to thicker cotton for $7.50, what is the deferred payment price of the blanket?

A. $19.95
B. $27.45
C. $59.85
D. $67.35

53. The local high school held a musical and raised $988.75 from admissions. If the tickets were $3.50 for adults and $1.75 for children and 335 tickets were sold, how many of the tickets were for adults and how many were for children?

A. 105 adult, 235 children
B. 132 adult, 124 children
C. 200 adult, 100 children
D. 230 adult, 105 children

54. The following table of index values for widgets is relative to 1980. If the price of widgets were $8 in 1960, what was the price of widgets in 2010?

Year	1970	1980	1990	2000	2010
Index	80	100	120	140	180

A. $12.50
B. $18
C. $22.50
D. $24.50

55. A family pays 360 payments of $902.43 on a house mortgage. The original loan was for $250,000. How much was the total interest paid on this loan?

   A. $65,145.55
   B. $68,512.50
   C. $70,450.55
   D. $74,874.80

56. If a credit card company charges 1% per month, what is the APR?

   A. 1.0%
   B. 12.0%
   C. 12.06%
   D. 14.36%

57. Solve the inequality: $-3x + 4 < 5x + 7$

   A. $x < \dfrac{3}{8}$

   B. $x > \dfrac{3}{8}$

   C. $x > -\dfrac{3}{8}$

   D. $x < -\dfrac{3}{8}$

58. If the nominal annual interest rate is 18%, what is the effective annual interest rate?

   A. 1.5%
   B. 19.56%
   C. 19.72%
   D. 21.6%

59. In baseball, a batting average is the number of hits divided by the number of times at bat rounded to 3 decimal places. What would the batting average be of a player who got 154 hits out of 403 at bats?

   A. 0.382
   B. 0.403
   C. 2.62
   D. 154

60. In the month of April, it rained a total of 22 days. What was the percentage of days that it rained for that month?

    A. 7.3%

    B. 72%

    C. 73%

    D. 79%

ANSWER KEY AND EXPLANATIONS

1. D	13. C	25. B	37. A	49. C
2. B	14. B	26. B	38. C	50. A
3. C	15. C	27. A	39. D	51. B
4. D	16. C	28. D	40. A	52. D
5. B	17. B	29. C	41. A	53. D
6. A	18. C	30. C	42. C	54. B
7. D	19. A	31. D	43. A	55. D
8. C	20. C	32. D	44. A	56. B
9. B	21. C	33. B	45. C	57. C
10. C	22. C	34. A	46. B	58. B
11. B	23. D	35. C	47. A	59. A
12. B	24. B	36. D	48. C	60. C

1. **The correct answer is D.** Find a common denominator and add the two fractions together:

$$= \frac{1}{3} + \frac{1}{4} + \frac{1}{4}$$

$$= \frac{1}{3}\left(\frac{4}{4}\right) + \frac{1}{4}\left(\frac{3}{3}\right) + \frac{1}{4}\left(\frac{3}{3}\right)$$

$$= \frac{4}{12} + \frac{3}{12} + \frac{3}{12}$$

$$= \frac{10}{12}$$

$$= \frac{5}{6}$$

Leon ate five sixths of a pie.

2. **The correct answer is B.** The lender owns a purchase made on installments until the full price is paid.

3. **The correct answer is C.** An amortized loan is a loan where payments are made each period, usually monthly, to pay off interest and principal.

4. **The correct answer is D.** We can solve using the effective interest rate for continuous interest which is $r_E = e^r - 1$:

$$r_E = e^{0.12} - 1$$
$$r_E = 0.1275$$

The effective interest rate is 12.75%.

5. **The correct answer is B.** The P/E ratio is the price-to-earnings ratio of a company's current share price compared to its per-share earnings.

6. **The correct answer is A.** The monthly interest rate is the APR ÷ 12, or monthly interest = 19.2 ÷ 12 = 1.6%.

7. **The correct answer is D.** Use the quadratic equation to solve:

$x = \dfrac{-b \pm \sqrt{b^2 - 4ac}}{2a}$ where $a = 3$, $b = -3$, and $c = \dfrac{1}{2}$.

$$x = \frac{-(-3) \pm \sqrt{(-3)^2 - 4(-3)\left(\frac{1}{2}\right)}}{2(3)}$$

$$x = \frac{3 \pm \sqrt{9 - 6}}{6}$$

$$x = \frac{3 \pm \sqrt{3}}{6}$$

Now solve for both the negative and positive:

$$x = \frac{3 \pm \sqrt{3}}{6} \qquad\qquad x = \frac{3 - \sqrt{3}}{6}$$

$$x = \frac{3}{6} + \frac{\sqrt{3}}{6} \qquad\qquad x = \frac{3}{6} - \frac{\sqrt{3}}{6}$$

$$x = \frac{1}{2} + \frac{\sqrt{3}}{6} \qquad\qquad x = \frac{1}{2} - \frac{\sqrt{3}}{6}$$

The solution is $x = \dfrac{1}{2} \pm \dfrac{\sqrt{3}}{6}$.

8. The correct answer is C. The *y*-axis label and values are missing.

9. The correct answer is B. If you graph (0, 1) and (1, 3), you will see that only the solution (–1, –1) falls on the line created by these two points. The other choices do not fall in the line created by (0, 1) and (1, 3).

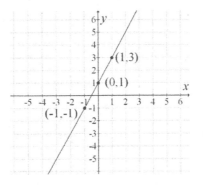

10. The correct answer is C. Being in the 75th percentile means that the boy is taller than 75% of boys his age.

11. The correct answer is B. First, evaluate the plot and determine the obvious points. For example, the line goes through the *y*-axis at 5 when $x = 0$, so we know (0, 5) is one of the line's points. If we evaluate the functions, we can see that answer choices A and C do not fit this point. The next point we can evaluate is the point where the line crosses the *x*-axis. At this point, we know that $y = 0$. Substitute 0 for *y* in answer choices B and D and solve for *x*:

B	D
$f(x) = 3x + 5$	$f(x) = 5x + 5$
$0 = 3x + 5$	$0 = 5x + 5$
$-5 = 3x$	$-5 = 5x$
$\dfrac{-5}{3} = x$	$\dfrac{-5}{5} = x$
$x \approx -1.67$	$x = -1$

The graph shows the line crossing the *x*-axis somewhere between –1 and –2, so the plot represents the function $f(x) = 3x + 5$ (choice B).

12. **The correct answer is B.** Rank the points from smallest to largest:

$$3, 3, 4, 4, 4, 5, 6, 7, 9$$

The median is the middle value, or 4. The mean or average is found by dividing the sum of the terms by the number of terms:

$$\text{avg} = \frac{3+3+4+4+4+5+6+7+9}{9}$$

$$= \frac{45}{9}$$

$$= 5$$

The median of the terms is 5. The difference between the mean and the median is $5 - 4 = 1$.

13. **The correct answer is C.** 2/20, n/30 is the correct notation for credit terms.

14. **The correct answer is B.** A promissory note is a contract between a borrower and a lender often required for a loan.

15. **The correct answer is C.** With this type of problem, the first steps should be to create as many equations as can be found in the given information. Using these equations, you can solve the problem. We know the probability for hitting a #4 prize balloon is 1 in 100, or 0.01. The probability for hitting a #3 prize balloon is 10 in 100, or 0.1. Using the equation for expected value, with the number of balloons as n_1 through n_4, we can create our first equation:

$$Ex_{balloons} = p_1 1 + p_2 2 + p_3 3 + p_4 4$$

$$1.5 = \left(\frac{n_1}{100}\right)1 + \left(\frac{n_2}{100}\right)2 + \left(\frac{10}{100}\right)3 + \left(\frac{1}{100}\right)4$$

$$1.5 = \left(\frac{n_1}{100}\right)1 + \left(\frac{n_2}{100}\right)2 + (0.1)3 + (0.01)4$$

$$1.5 = \left(\frac{n_1}{100}\right)1 + \left(\frac{n_2}{50}\right) + 0.34$$

$$1.16 = \left(\frac{n_1}{100}\right)1 + \left(\frac{n_2}{50}\right)$$

We also know that the total number of balloons = 100, so we can create a second equation:

$$total = n_1 + n_2 + n_3 + n_4$$
$$100 = n_1 + n_2 + 10 + 1$$
$$100 = n_1 + n_2 + 11$$
$$89 = n_1 + n_2$$

Now we have two equations and two unknowns. We can solve the second equation for n_1:

$$89 = n_1 + n_2$$
$$n_1 = 89 - n_2$$

Substitute this value of n_1 into the first equation:

$$1.16 = \left(\frac{89 - n_2}{100}\right) + \left(\frac{n_2}{50}\right)$$
$$1.16 = \frac{89}{100} - \frac{n_2}{100} + \frac{n_2}{50}$$
$$1.16 = 0.89 - \frac{n_2}{100} + \frac{2n_2}{100}$$
$$1.16 = 0.89 + \frac{(2-1)n_2}{100}$$
$$1.16 = 0.89 + \frac{n_2}{100}$$
$$1.16 - 0.89 = \frac{n_2}{100}$$
$$0.27 = \frac{n_2}{100}$$
$$n_2 = 27$$

Now that we know we have 27 #2 prize balloons, we can solve using the second equation:

$$89 = n_1 + n_2$$
$$89 = n_1 + 27$$
$$89 - 27 = n_1$$
$$n_1 = 62$$

So, she must prepare 62 #1 prize balloons and 27 #2 prize balloons.

You can check just to make sure that the total of all balloons does, in fact, equal 100:

$$62 + 27 + 10 + 1 = 100$$

16. **The correct answer is C.** We can solve using the calculation for the future value of an ordinary annuity equation:

$$FV_{OA} = PMT \left[\frac{\left(1 + \dfrac{r}{m}\right)^{mn} - 1}{\dfrac{r}{m}} \right]$$

Where $r = 0.08$, $m = 1$, $t = 10$, and $PMT = 85,000$

$$FV_{OA} = 85,000 \left[\frac{\left(1 + \dfrac{0.08}{1}\right)^{(1)(10)} - 1}{\dfrac{0.08}{1}} \right]$$

$$= 85,000 \left[\frac{\left(1.08\right)^{(1)(10)} - 1}{\dfrac{0.08}{1}} \right]$$

$$= 85,000 \left[\frac{\left(1.08\right)^{(1)(10)} - 1}{\dfrac{0.08}{1}} \right]$$

$$= 85,000 \left[14.48565 \right]$$

$$= 1,231,357.81$$

The future value in his account will be \$1,231,357.81.

17. The correct answer is B. We first need to determine the total number of possible throws:

1	TTT
2	TTH
3	THT
4	THH
5	HTT
6	HTH
7	HHT
8	HHH

We can see that there are 8 possible tosses of three coins. Only one of the tosses in 8 will come up "heads, heads, heads" so $1/8 = 12.5$ percent.

18. The correct answer is C. First, calculate the markdown. $9,500 - 6,950 = 2,550$.

Using the equation for markdown,

$$\text{Markdown \%} = \frac{\text{Markdown Price}}{\text{Original Selling Price}} \times 100 \text{, we can solve:}$$

$$MD\% = \frac{2,550}{9,500}(100)$$
$$= 26.84$$
$$= 27\%$$

The markdown is 27%.

19. **The correct answer is A.** Use the equation for total cost $C(x) = mx + F$, where $C(x) =$ total cost, $m =$ variable cost, and $F =$ fixed cost:

$$4.0(10,000) + 9,800 = 3.5(10,000) + (9,800 + x)$$
$$40,000 + 9,800 = 35,000 + 9,800 + x$$
$$49,800 = 44,800 + x$$
$$49,800 - 44,800 = x$$
$$5,000 = x$$

The manufacturer can spend up to $5,000 for additional fixed costs.

20. **The correct solution is C.** Use the equation Selling Price = Cost (1 + % Markup), and solve for cost:

$$185 = \text{Cost}(1 + 0.85)$$
$$\text{Cost} = \frac{185}{1.85}$$
$$\text{Cost} = 100$$

The cost is $100.

21. **The correct answer is C.** The equation for current ratio is:

$$\text{Index Number} = \frac{\text{Current Value of the Indicator}}{\text{Total Current Liabilities}}$$

We know a 2:1 ratio means there are twice the current assets as total current liabilities. A ratio of 2:1 is considered healthy.

22. **The correct answer is C.** The 50th percentile is the center value. Rank the prices from smallest to largest, and $17.50 is the center value.

23. The correct answer is D. Use the equation for index number to calculate the current price in 2000:

$$\text{Index Number} = \frac{\text{Current Value of the Indicator}}{\text{Base Period Value of the Indicator}} \times 100$$

$$250 = \frac{x}{12}(100)$$
$$x = \frac{250(12)}{100}$$
$$x = \frac{3,000}{100}$$
$$x = 30$$

The price in 2000 was $30.

24. The correct answer is B. Use the equation to solve for the depreciation:

$$\text{Depreciation} = \frac{\text{Cost} - \text{Residual Value}}{\text{Estimated Useful Life}}$$

$$D = \frac{100,000 - 20,000}{8}$$
$$D = \frac{80,000}{8}$$
$$D = 10,000$$

The depreciation is $10,000.

25. The correct answer is B. Solve the first equation for y:

$$2x + y = 5$$
$$y = 5 - 2x$$

Substitute this value of y into the second equation:

$$5x + 5(5 - 2x) = 5$$
$$5x + 25 - 10x = 5$$
$$-5x = 5 - 25$$
$$-5x = -20$$
$$x = 4$$

Substitute this value of x into the first equation:

$$2(4) + y = 5$$
$$8 + y = 5$$
$$y = 5 - 8$$
$$y = -3$$

The solution is (4, –3).

26. The correct answer is B. A 3% discount is $(0.03)(1,000) = 30$. We then subtract this from 1,000. $1,000 - 30 = 970$. The discounted price is $970.

27. The correct answer is A. The equation Property Tax = Tax Rate × Total Assessed Value can be used to calculate the Budget:

$$\text{Tax} = (0.0648)(32,500,000)$$
$$= 2,106,000$$

The city will raise $2,106,000.

28. The correct answer is D. Although the market plays a strong role in the assessed value for property, the government sets the final assessed value.

29. The correct answer is C. For 1,500 widgets, let $x = 1,500$ and solve:

$$C(1,500) = 0.17(1,500) + 50,000$$
$$= 50,255$$

The total cost of manufacturing 1,500 widgets is $50,255.

30. The correct answer is C. Use the quadratic equation to solve:

$x = \dfrac{-b \pm \sqrt{b^2 - 4ac}}{2a}$, where $a = 1$, $b = -6$, and $c = 5$.

$$x = \frac{-(-6) \pm \sqrt{(-6)^2 - 4(1)(5)}}{2(1)}$$
$$x = \frac{6 \pm \sqrt{6 - 20}}{2}$$
$$x = \frac{6 \pm \sqrt{16}}{2}$$
$$x = \frac{6 \pm 4}{2}$$

Now solve for both the negative and positive:

$$x = \frac{6+4}{2} \qquad\qquad x = \frac{6-4}{2}$$
$$x = 5 \qquad\qquad x = 1$$

The solution is $x = 5$ and $x = 1$.

31. The correct answer is D. To solve, evaluate the following equation for $C(x) = 16,200$, $x = 10,000$ and $m = 1.45$ and find the value of the fixed cost:

$$C(x) = m(x) + Fc$$
$$16,200 = 1.45(10,000) + Fc$$
$$Fc = 16,200 - 1.45(10,000)$$
$$Fc = 16,200 - 14,500$$
$$Fc = 1,700$$

The fixed cost is $1,700.

32. **The correct answer is D.** To find the solution, we need only to set the two equations equal to each other and solve for x:

$$C(x) = R(x)$$
$$1.2x + 1{,}274 = 6x$$
$$1.2x - 6x = -1{,}274$$
$$(1.2 - 6)x = -1{,}274$$
$$-4.8x = -1{,}274$$
$$x = 265.4167$$

To break even, they need to make just a little more than 265 units, so they need 266 units.

33. **The correct answer is B.** Use the equation for standard error $SE_{\bar{x}} = \dfrac{\sigma}{\sqrt{n}}$ to solve for n:

$$2 = \frac{20}{\sqrt{n}}$$
$$\sqrt{n} = \frac{20}{2}$$
$$\sqrt{n} = \frac{20}{2}$$
$$\sqrt{n} = 10$$
$$\left(\sqrt{n}\right)^2 = 10^2$$
$$n = 100$$

There are 100 data points.

34. **The correct answer is A.** To find the solution, set the two equations equal to each other and solve for x:

$$C(x) = R(x)$$
$$1.5x + 11{,}700 = 4x$$
$$1.5x - 4x = -11{,}700$$
$$(1.5 - 4)x = -11{,}700$$
$$-2.5x = -11{,}700$$
$$x = 4{,}680$$

To break even they need to make just more than 4,680 units. Now calculate $R(x) = 4(4{,}680) = 18{,}720$.

35. The correct answer is C. To solve, multiply the base year expenses by the 2014 percentage: (0.85)(243,000) = 206,550.

36. The correct answer is D. To solve the linear equation, add 10 to both sides and then divide by 3:

$$3x - 10 = 23$$
$$3x - 10 + 10 = 23 + 10$$
$$3x = 33$$
$$\frac{1}{3}(3x) = \frac{1}{3}(33)$$
$$\left(\frac{3}{3}\right)x = \frac{33}{3}$$
$$x = 11$$

The solution is 11.

37. The correct answer is A. If 9% of the budget goes to food, then (0.09)(3,000) = $270 per month.

38. The correct answer is C. Use the equation for linear interpolation:

$$y_2 = \frac{\left(x_2 - x_1\right)\left(y_3 - y_1\right)}{\left(x_3 - x_1\right)}$$

$$x = \frac{(7 - 1(89 - 45)}{(15 - 1)} + 45$$
$$x = \frac{(65)(44)}{(14)} + 45$$
$$x = 18.857 + 45$$
$$x = 63.86$$

The interpolated value is 63.86.

39. The correct answer is D. Use a conversion table form to convert and cancel units:

2,940 ~~euros~~	1.42 dollars	1 ~~week~~
1 ~~week~~	1 ~~euro~~	7 days

$$= \frac{(2,940)(1.42)\,\text{euro}}{7\,\text{days}} = 596.40 \text{ dollars per day}$$

The businesswoman spent $586.40 per day.

40. The correct answer is A. A Type I error is when you believe something is true and it is not. The researcher believed his data showed a significant difference when there was none.

41. The correct answer is A. Use the equation to make the conversion:

$$18 = \frac{5}{9}(F - 32)$$
$$18 = (0.556)F - (0.556)(32)$$
$$18 = 0.556F - 17.778$$
$$0.556F = 18 + 17.778$$
$$0.556F = 35.778$$
$$F = 64.34$$

The temperature is 64.3° Fahrenheit.

42. The correct answer is C. Use the weighted average equation:

$$GPA = \frac{(3)(A) + (3)(B) + (4)(B) + (4)(C) + (2)(A)}{3 + 3 + 4 + 4 + 2}$$
$$= \frac{(3)(4) + (3)(3) + (4)(3) + (4)(2) + (2)(4)}{3 + 3 + 4 + 4 + 2}$$
$$= \frac{12 + 9 + 12 + 8 + 8}{16}$$
$$= \frac{49}{16}$$
$$= 3.06$$

Milo's GPA would be 3.06.

43. The correct answer is A. Use the following equation to calculate the stock yield:

$$\text{Stock Yield} = \frac{\text{Annual Dividend per Share}}{\text{Current Share Price}}$$

Solve:

$$SY = \frac{2}{45}$$
$$SY = 0.044$$
$$SY = 4.4\%$$

The stock yield is 4.4%.

44. The correct answer is A. Lowering the fixed or variable cost of manufacture will decrease the number of units to break even. Increasing the price (choice B) will lower the number of units it takes to break even, but the increased price could slow sales. With reduced manufacturing costs, the sale price will not have to be lowered (choice C), so the time it takes to break even will be reduced.

45. The correct answer is C. Use the equation $FV = PV\left(1+\dfrac{r}{m}\right)^{mt}$ to solve for the future value:

$$FV = 1{,}800\left(1+\frac{0.095}{12}\right)^{(12)(8)}$$
$$= 1{,}800(1+0.0079167)^{96}$$
$$= 1{,}800(1.0079167)^{96}$$
$$= 1{,}800(2.1319)$$
$$= 3{,}837.41$$

The future value is $3,837.41.

46. **The correct answer is B.** We can solve using the calculation for an ordinary annuity present value:

$$PV_{OA} = PMT\left[\frac{1 - \frac{1}{\left(1+\frac{r}{m}\right)^{tm}}}{\frac{r}{m}}\right]$$

Where $r = 0.12$, $m = 12$, $t = 2$, and $PMT = \$50$:

$$PV_{OA} = PMT\left[\frac{1 - \frac{1}{\left(1+\frac{0.12}{12}\right)^{(2)(12)}}}{\frac{0.12}{12}}\right]$$

$$= 50\left[\frac{1 - \frac{1}{(1.01)^{24}}}{0.01}\right]$$

$$= 50\left[\frac{1 - \frac{1}{1.12697}}{0.01}\right]$$

$$= 50\left[\frac{0.212434}{0.01}\right]$$

$$= 1062.17$$

The present value of the gift is $1,062.17.

47. **The correct answer is A.** The distribution is normal, so we know that half of the students most likely scored above the average, 78, so choice B is incorrect. The correct percentage of students that scored between 57 and 99, or mean ± 3 standard deviations, is 99.7%, thus choice C is incorrect. It is possible that someone scored outside the ± 3 sigma limits and could have scored a 100 on the test, thus choice D is incorrect. The distribution of the grades was normal, so the students can correctly assume that 68% of the students scored between the mean ± 1 standard, 71 and 85.

48. The correct answer is C. We can solve using the calculation for an ordinary annuity equation for payments:

$$PMT_{OA} = PV \left[\frac{\frac{r}{m}}{\left(1 + \frac{r}{m}\right)^{mn} - 1} \right] \left(1 + \frac{r}{m}\right)^{mn}$$

Where $r = 0.10$, $m = 12$, $t = 3$, and $PV = \$20,000 - \$5,000 = \$15,000$:

$$PMT_{OA} = 15,000 \left[\frac{\frac{0.1}{12}}{\left(1 + \frac{0.1}{12}\right)^{(12)(3)} - 1} \right] \left(1 + \frac{0.1}{12}\right)^{(12)(3)}$$

$$PV_{OA} = 15,000 \left[\frac{0.008333}{\left(1 + 0.008333\right)^{36} - 1} \right] \left(1 + 0.008333\right)^{36}$$

$$= 15,000 \left[\frac{0.008333}{\left(1.008333\right)^{36} - 1} \right] \left(1.008333\right)^{36}$$

$$= 15,000 \left[\frac{0.008333}{0.348166} \right] 1.348166$$

$$= 15,000 (0.023934) 1.348166$$

$$= 484.01$$

The monthly payment of $484.01 will be needed.

49. The correct answer is C. Use the equation to solve for salvage value:

$$\text{Depreciation} = \frac{\text{Cost Residual} - \text{Value}}{\text{Estimated Useful Life}}$$

$$2,000 = \frac{20,000 - x}{7}$$

$$(2,000)(7) = 20,000 - x$$

$$14,000 = 20,000 - x$$

$$14,000 - 20,000 = -x$$

$$-6,000 = -x$$

$$x = 6,000$$

The salvage value is $6,000.

50. The correct answer is A. Use the equation $i = PVrt$ to solve for i.

$$i = (500)(0.08)(5) = \$200.$$

51. The correct answer is B. We can solve using the equation for amortization:

$$PMT_{Amort} = \frac{PV\left(\dfrac{r}{m}\right)}{1 - \left(1 + \dfrac{r}{m}\right)^{-mt}}$$

Where $r = 0.055$, $m = 1$, $t = 15$, and $PMT = 265{,}000 - 25{,}000 = 240{,}000$:

$$
\begin{aligned}
PMT_{Amort} &= \frac{PV\left(\dfrac{r}{m}\right)}{1 - \left(+\dfrac{r}{m}\right)^{-mt}} \\[2mm]
&= \frac{240{,}000\left(\dfrac{0.055}{12}\right)}{1 - \left(1 + \dfrac{0.055}{12}\right)^{-(12)(15)}} \\[2mm]
&= \frac{240{,}000(0.00458333)}{1 - (1.00458333)^{-180}} \\[2mm]
&= \frac{1{,}099.92}{1 - 0.439061786} \\[2mm]
&= 1{,}961.00
\end{aligned}
$$

The monthly payment is \$1,961.00.

52. The correct answer is D. Use the equation Deferred Payment Price = Total of All Payments + Down Payment to solve.

$$DPP = 3(19.95) + 7.50 = \$67.35.$$

53. The correct answer is D. To solve this problem, let a = number of adult tickets sold and c = number of children's tickets sold. We know $1.75c + 3.5a = 988.75$ and $c + a = 335$:

First, solve the second equation for c:

$$c + a = 335$$
$$c = 335 - a$$

Substitute this value into the first equation:

$$1.75(335 - a) + 3.5a = 988.75$$
$$586.25 - 1.75a + 3.5a = 988.75$$
$$(-1.75 + 3.5)a = 988.75 - 586.25$$
$$1.75a = 402.5$$
$$a = 230$$

Use this value of a and substitute it into the second equation:

$$c + a = 335$$
$$c + 230 = 335$$
$$c = 335 - 230$$
$$c = 105$$

The high school sold 230 adult tickets and 105 children's tickets.

54. The correct answer is B. First, solve using the equation

$$\text{Index Number} = \frac{\text{Current Value}}{\text{Base Period Value}} \times 100 \text{ for 1970 to get the}$$

1980 base value:

$$80 = \frac{8}{x}(100)$$
$$x = \frac{(10)(100)}{80}$$
$$x = 10$$

The base value for 1980 is $10. Using this value, we can find the price in 2010:

$$180 = \frac{x}{10}(100)$$
$$x = \frac{(10)(180)}{100}$$
$$x = 18$$

The price of widgets in 2010 was $18.

55. The correct answer is D. First, calculate the total amount paid on the loan:

$$(360)(902.43) = 324{,}874.8$$

Next, find the total amount of interest:

$$\text{total} = 324{,}874.80 - 250{,}000$$
$$= 74{,}874.80$$

The total interest paid is $74,874.80.

56. The correct answer is B. The APR is the monthly rate multiplied by 12, or 1% × 12 = 12%.

57. The correct answer is C. To solve this inequality, you need to isolate x on one side of the equation:

$$-3x + 4 < 5x + 7$$
$$-3x - 5x + 4 < 5x - 5x + 7$$
$$(-3 - 5)x + 4 < 7$$
$$-8x + 4 < 7$$
$$-8x + 4 - 4 < 7 - 4$$
$$-8x < 3$$
$$x > -\frac{3}{8}$$

Remember that you must flip the inequality sign if you multiply or divide by a negative number.

58. The correct answer is B. To solve, use the equation:

$$r_E = \left(1 + \frac{r}{m}\right)^m - 1$$
$$r_E = \left(1 + \frac{0.18}{12}\right)^{12} - 1$$
$$r_E = (1 + 0.015)^{12} - 1$$
$$r_E = (1.015)^{12} - 1$$
$$r_E = 0.195618$$

The effective interest rate is 19.56%.

59. The correct answer is A. Divide 403 into 154 and round to three decimal places:

$$= \frac{54}{403}$$
$$= 0.382133$$
$$= 0.382$$

The batting average is 0.382.

60. **The correct answer is C.** There are 30 days in the month of April. If it rained for 22 days, then the percentage of days that it rained is:

$$= \frac{22}{30} \times 100$$
$$= 73.33\%$$

It rained 73% of the days in April.

Like what you see? Get unlimited access to Peterson's full catalog of DSST practice tests, instructional videos, flashcards and more for **75% off the first month!** Go to **www.petersons.com/testprep/dsst** and use coupon code **DSST2020** at checkout. Offer expires July 1, 2021.

CPSIA information can be obtained
at www.ICGtesting.com
Printed in the USA
JSHW041455300622
27690JS00007B/181

9 780768 944396